BBIN—A Post-SAARC Phenomenon

Unlocking the Potential for Energy Cooperation

BBIN—A Post-SAARC Phenomenon

Unlocking the Potential for Energy Cooperation

SIMI MEHTA

KW Publishers Pvt Ltd
New Delhi

Indian Council of World Affairs
New Delhi

ISBN 978-81-984037-0-4 Hardback

Published in India by Kalpana Shukla

KW Publishers Pvt Ltd
4676/21, First Floor, Ansari Road
Daryaganj, New Delhi 110 002
Phone: +91 11 43528107
Marketing: kw@kwpub.in
Editorial: production@kwpub.in
Website: www.kwpub.in

Printed and bound in India
Quiinkit Infotech Pvt. Ltd., Gurugram

Contents

Preface

This book titled '*BBIN—A Post-SAARC Phenomenon: Unlocking the Potential for Energy Cooperation*' examines the emergence and evolution of the Bangladesh-Bhutan-India-Nepal (BBIN) framework as a pragmatic sub-regional alternative to the broader but often stagnant SAARC mechanism. It focuses on unlocking the untapped potential of energy cooperation in the region—an area ripe for strategic collaboration yet hindered by infrastructural and political challenges.

Grounded in the theoretical foundations of sub-regionalism, the book analyses the shifting patterns of regional integration through trade, connectivity, and energy policy. It draws on extensive empirical research, secondary sources, and a wide range of expert interviews conducted across the BBIN countries, offering valuable insights into on-ground realities, policy thinking, and institutional preparedness. These interviews serve as an important supplement, reflecting nuanced perspectives from key stakeholders, scholars, and practitioners in the field. Their profound analytical insights are certain to serve as a valuable tool to support a strengthened and united sub-region; becoming further relevant due to the prevailing geopolitical flux. While this book delineates the practical challenges that come in the way of unlocking the energy cooperation capacity, it also provides responses and potential solutions that will help the four nations tackle them head-on. Such problem-solving approaches offers itself as a crucial guide to current and future policies as well as actions to be taken by the political leader of the respective countries.

This book espouses that cohesion in the energy sector between the BBIN countries will provide the much needed sheen in the Golden Quadrangle and promote quadruple objectives of security, prosperity, stability and peace in the sub-region.

In a time of heightened climate concerns and energy insecurity, this book argues that BBIN cooperation—particularly in the renewable and cross-border energy domains—offers a strategic pathway toward sustainable growth and collective resilience. The aim is to inform and inspire policymakers, researchers, and development professionals working on South Asian regionalism, energy governance, and cross-border collaboration. The arrangement of the chapters suggest the immediacy of the challenges that confront the BBIN sub-region in the energy sector. Since identifying the challenges implies the need to explore the remedial measures extensive analysis through review of literature and findings through fieldwork provides necessary policy recommendations comprising insights from the practitioners, policy makers and academic experts.

I earnestly hope that this volume will spark further conversations and contribute meaningfully to policy frameworks across the region.

Tables

Abbreviations

ADB	Asian Development Bank
AL	Awami League (political party in Bangladesh)
ASEAN	Association of Southeast Asian Nations
ATS	Associated cross border Transmission System
BBIN	Bangladesh, Bhutan, India, Nepal
BNP	Bangladesh Nationalist Party
BRI	Belt and Road Initiative
BU	Billion Units (unit of electricity)
CBET	Cross Border Electricity Trade
CEA	Central Electricity Authority (India)
CERC	Central Electricity Regulatory Commission (India)
CES	Continental Europe Synchronous Area
CH4	Methane
CO2	Carbon Dioxide
COP21	21st Conference of Parties
COVID-19	Coronavirus Disease 2019
CPTC	Cross Border Power Transmission Company Pvt. Ltd.
D/C	Direct Current
DFQF	Duty-Free Quota-Free
ECT	Energy Charter Treaty
EEC	European Economic Community

EITI	Extractive Industries Transparency Initiative
EPF	Electric Power Forum
EU	European Union
GDP	Gross Domestic Product
GHG	Greenhouse Gas
GHGs	Greenhouse Gases
GJ	Gigajoules
GLOFs	Glacial Lake Outburst Floods
GMS	Greater Mekong Subregion
GW	Gigawatt
GWh	Gigawatt hour
HEP	Hydroelectric Project
HFO	Heavy Fuel Oil
HVDC	High Voltage Direct Current
IBA	Initial Business Analysis
ICT	Information and Communication Technology
IEA	International Energy Agency
IFC	International Finance Corporation
IEX	Indian Energy Exchange
IL&FS	Infrastructure Leasing & Financial Services Limited
IMF	International Monetary Fund
INDC	Intended Nationally Determined Contribution
INR	Indian Rupee
IRENA	International Renewable Energy Agency
ISA	International Solar Alliance
IPP	Independent Power Producer
JWG	Joint Working Group
KV	Kilovolts (unit of voltage)
kWh	Kilowatt hour
LDCs	Least Developed Countries
MJ	Megajoules

MNRE	Ministry of New and Renewable Energy
MoU	Memorandum of Understanding
MSME	Micro, Small, and Medium Enterprise
Mt	Metric Tonnes
MtCO2e	Million Metric Tons of Carbon Dioxide Equivalent
MW	Megawatt
MVA	Motor Vehicles Agreement
NAPCC	National Action Plan on Climate Change
NAFTA	North American Free Trade Area
NATO	North Atlantic Treaty Organization
NC	Nepali Congress (political party in Nepal)
NDC	Nationally Determined Contribution
NDCs	Nationally Determined Contributions
NEA	Nepal Electricity Authority
NSM	National Solar Mission
OECD	Organisation for Economic Cooperation and Development
PJ	Petajoules
PPP	Public Private Partnership
PPA	Power Purchase Agreement
PTC	Power Trading Corporation
PTCN	Power Transmission Company Nepal Ltd.
PV	Photovoltaic
RD&D	Research, Demonstration and Development
RE	Renewable Energy
RETA	Regional Technical Assistance
RETs	Renewable Energy Technologies
RGoB	Royal Government of Bhutan
RIIA	Royal Institute of International Affairs
RoR	Run of the River
ROR	Run of River

RPOs	Renewable Purchase Obligations
Rs.	Indian Rupees
SADF	SAARC Development Fund
SAGQ	South Asia Growth Quadrangle
SAARC	South Asian Association for Regional Cooperation
SAFTA	South Asian Free Trade Area
SAPP	Southern African Power Pool
SARI/Energy	South Asia Regional Initiative for Energy
SATAT	Sustainable Alternative Towards Affordable Transportation
SAU	South Asian University
SDF	SAARC Development Fund
SDG	Sustainable Development Goals
SEMAN	Solar Electric Manufacturer's Association Nepal
SASEC	South Asian Sub-Regional Economic Cooperation
SJVNL	Satluj Jal Vidyut Nigam Limited
SREDA	Sustainable and Renewable Energy Development Authority
TES	Total Energy Supply
TFEC	Total Final Electricity Consumption
TJ	Terajoule
UML	United Marxist Leninist Party (political party in Nepal)
UNFCCC	United Nations Framework Convention on Climate Change
USD	United States Dollar
WASH	Water, Sanitation and Hygiene
WMO	World Meteorological Organization
WTO	World Trade Organization

1
Introduction

Unilateralism has ceded its space to multilateralism in the discourse of international relations. Regional and sub-regional cooperation plays an important role in mitigating regional conflicts and dissonance and is often desired for regional peace, growth, stability, and development.

The need for increased economic cooperation among geographically contiguous countries has been a dominant feature of the global political economy ever since the emergence of the European Economic Community (EEC) in the late 1940s and the Association of Southeast Asian Nations (ASEAN) in the 1960s. The rationale for such cooperation has been strengthened further in the 1990s by the emergence of regional trading blocs like the European Union (EU) and the North American Free Trade Area (NAFTA).

The 1980s marked the most significant achievement of the vision to have a regional grouping for South Asia. Seven countries, including Bangladesh, Bhutan, India, the Maldives, Nepal, Pakistan, and Sri Lanka, joined hands to establish the South Asian Association for Regional Cooperation (SAARC) in 1985. The Islamic Republic of Afghanistan joined SAARC as a full-fledged member in 2007. The desire to promote peace, harmony, and socio-economic growth and thereby build trust among the countries overshadowed the uneasy relations between India and Pakistan. The contributing factors for this included the recognition and importance placed upon common history, traditions, and culture, as well as a contiguous geography and socio-economic proximity.

The goals of SAARC included the promotion of the welfare of the population of South Asia; strengthening collective self-reliance; promotion of active collaboration and mutual assistance in various fields like agriculture, rural development, telecommunications, meteorology, and health and population activities, etc. by sharing the available resources; and fostering cooperation with other international and regional organisations. It also elicited regular Summit meetings between political leaders and set up an institutional framework to discuss the modalities and opportunities for cooperation between the member states. The leaders underscored five basic principles as the basis of cooperation, which included: sovereign equality, territorial integrity, political independence, non-interference in internal affairs of the member states, and mutual benefit. Overall, regional cooperation in the form of SAARC sought to complement the bilateral and multilateral relations of SAARC member states. In pursuance of this, Article VII of the SAARC Charter highlights that should there be project(s) that require implementation, the Standing Committee may set up Action Committees, involving more than two but not all member states, where the project(s) may be realised.

While the establishment of SAARC has not resulted in the creation of a perfect regional organisation, nonetheless, it has undertaken important small steps towards that path. This regional forum, with the aim of promoting cooperation in economic, social, cultural, and scientific fields, as affirmed by the Charter, opened new opportunities for trade and investment, knowledge exchange, and people-to-people connect for the region. Some of these are discussed below.

Demonstrating its seriousness on the issue of easing trade flows with other countries, in 2008, India became the first developing country to provide Duty- Free Quota- Free (DFQF) access for the least developed countries (LDCs) of SAARC, which gradually increased to 34 in 2017 (Ministry of Commerce, Government of India, 2017). DFQF access was an outcome of the WTO Hong Kong Ministerial Meeting held in December 2005.

In December 1995, SAARC introduced the South Asian Free Trade Area (SAFTA) to boost trade between the member states, emphasising that there was a need to understand the South Asian Free Zone Exchange. The contract was signed at the 12th Summit, which was held in Islamabad in January 2004. It emphasised that SAFTA would "act as a stimulus to the strengthening of national and SAARC economic resilience, and the development of the national economies of the Member States by expanding investment and production opportunities, trade, and foreign exchange earnings as well as the development of economic and technological cooperation (SAARC, 2004)." In December 2005, Government of India approved SAFTA and flagged it for its official launch on January 1, 2006, when it was hoped that all participating countries would lower interest rates by the 2016 deadline.

At the 14th SAARC Summit held in New Delhi on April 3-4, 2007, the member states decided to set up the SAARC Food Bank, which shall have a reserve of food grains to be maintained by each member state, consisting of either wheat or rice or a combination of both as the assessed share of the country. The objectives of the SAARC Food Bank are to act as a regional food security reserve for the member countries during normal time food shortages and emergencies like natural disasters, floods, earthquakes, etc.; provide regional support to national food security efforts; foster intercountry partnerships and regional integration; and solve regional food shortages through collective action (SAARC, 2007a). This will supplement national efforts to provide food security to the people of the region (Department of Food and Public Distribution, Government of India, n.d.). The five countries that have benefitted from this decision include Afghanistan, Bangladesh, Bhutan, Nepal, and the Maldives.

On August 3, 2008, the SAARC member states signed an agreement in Colombo to establish the SAARC Development Fund (SDF), and this was subsequently inaugurated at the 16th SAARC Summit organised in

Thimphu, Bhutan, in April 2010. Governed by the need to create a sound, adequate, and predictable funding mechanism for SAARC to facilitate undertaking sub-regional and regional programmes and projects, the Fund would help serve these ends and would constitute a new and unique South Asian character. The Fund was intended to improve quality of life and accelerate economic growth, social progress, and poverty alleviation in the region (SAARC, 2008a; Export-Import Bank of India, 2014). The Fund acts as an umbrella institutional entity to finance projects and programmes across the SAARC member countries. The Fund itself comprises three windows: social, economic and infrastructure, wherein the highest number of programmes belong to the social window category. Some of the projects under the ambit of the social window include Water, Sanitation and Hygiene (WASH) and promoting maternal and child health.

The SAARC Arbitration Council is an initiative to provide a legal forum for the member states for fair and efficient settlement of commercial, investment, and other disputes. The agreement to set up the SAARC Arbitration Council was entered into on November 13, 2005, at a meeting of the Foreign Affairs Ministers of all member states in Dhaka. It is one of the specialised bodies of SAARC, set up as an inter-governmental body authorised to provide a legal framework or forum within the region for fair and effective settlement of industrial, commercial, trade, investment banking, and other such issues and disputes, as may be referred to it by the member states and their people (SAARC Summit, 2011), with the aim to create conditions favourable for fostering greater investment by investors of one member state in the territory of another member state (SAARC, 2005).

On August 3, 2008, in Colombo, the SAARC member states sought to achieve and enhance coordination and cooperation among themselves in the fields of standardisation and conformity assessment; and aimed to develop harmonised standards for the region to facilitate intra-regional trade and to have access in the global market. To this end, they agreed to create the South Asian Regional Standards Organisation (SARSO) (SAARC, 2008b).

The main aim of SARSO is to deal with trade-related standards and harness the major potential for greater coordination of such standards to support trade growth in South Asia and universally for SAARC countries. It came into effect from August 25, 2011, after approval by all SAARC countries. By reviewing other relevant standardisation organisations, their methods and achievements, SARSO can adopt the tools and necessary approaches to achieve its goals and those of SAARC. The SARSO is positioned to create strong and effective structures for the harmonisation of trade standards to facilitate economic growth and development in South Asia (Cote, 2016).

Apart from these tangible asset creations, SAARC has also focused on encouraging cultural and people-to-people contacts. The progress in this sector has been healthy. The establishment of the South Asian University (SAU), a higher education institution centred in New Delhi, India, is reflective of encouraging cultural contacts and is another achievement by the member states.

The establishment of the SAU fulfils the need to provide a forum where academicians, scholars, researchers, and gifted students of SAARC can work together in the service of human advancement with a commitment to social justice that will advance a sense of South Asian community by bringing together the future generations of South Asians in a common pursuit of quality education and prepare them for the challenges of the time. It recognises the need to offer world-class education, comparable to the best universities in the world (SAARC, 2007b).

The agreement to establish the SAU was entered into on April 4, 2007, and this international university was formally established in 2010. The SAU is a significant step towards promoting regional development in the area of higher education. The university attracts students from all member nations, and its degrees are recognised by all eight SAARC countries. Tuition fee is heavily subsidised, and compensation packages have been designed to attract high quality faculty. "While SAARC may constantly be engaged in resolving the political and economic dilemmas amongst its members with limited success, optimists view the cooperation on education as one of the few achievements of SAARC. It may also be a catalyst for the regional integration process endowed with democratic ideals, a commitment to tolerance, multicultural and secular co-existence, and with a critical and scientific outlook—would provide leadership not only in their own countries but throughout the region.

The university aims to create a centre of excellence and produce leaders who identify themselves as citizens of the region with a common vision of success for both their home country and the neighbours", as attracting talent from the neighbourhood would nurture future ambassadors for its shared values (Ravi, 2014).

With the COVID-19 pandemic hitting the world, the Indian government proposed an emergency fund for COVID-19 for the SAARC member countries (Press Information Bureau, 2020). This step by the Indian government reiterated the importance of the organisation in ensuring collaboration and cooperation in the region. Apart from the emergency fund proposed by India, the government of India also spelt out several other steps that would help in combating the disease better. These included leveraging the facilities of the SAARC Disaster Management Centre and creating a common research platform to coordinate research related to the control of epidemics. Further, India also offered to share its disease surveillance software with its neighbours (Ibid.).

Despite all efforts, the South Asian regionalism failed to bring about significant change in trade, power, infrastructural relations, and technical harmonisation between the member states and harness their objectives to their advantage (Chaturvedi et al., 2015). The persisting history of friction and conflict, mistrust, and hostility among member states, including armed conflicts and religious and ethnic strife, have further hindered regional integration and dwarfed the relatively few successes cited above (Ahmed and Ghani, 2008; Niaz, 2022; Delinić, 2011). The initial role of the South Asian Association for Regional Cooperation (SAARC) as the representative of South Asian countries remained declaratory without delivering tangible political or economic benefits (Rao, 2012).

Despite the potential for growth through increased flow of labour, capital, and goods, the region's political and economic problems have limited the effectiveness of SAARC as an integrating body (Rao, 2012). While individually, some nations of SAARC have registered and continue to register high growth rates, the region, as a whole, continues to lag behind and makes South Asia the least integrated region of the world in terms of trade, people-to-people contact, cross-border investments, and exchange of ideas, among others (Export-Import Bank of India, 2014; World Bank, n.d.). This lack of integration translated into trade within the South Asian region increasing by only $23.04 billion of total trade from 2010 to 2022 (De, 2023). The major reasons for low intra-regional trade include higher transaction costs for those member states trading less with one another and lengthy time associated with the trade of goods and services due to procedural complexities exaggerated by excessive documentation requirements, informal trade; poor intra-regional connectivity; supply side constraints and weak productive capacity; and inadequacies of trade-related infrastructure, trade finance, and trade information, etc. (De, 2011; Export-Import Bank of India, 2014). Lack of access to trade finance has been a major barrier in intra-regional trade across various regional organisations (WTO, 2013). Chaturvedi et al. (2015) and Sawhney and Kumar (2008) highlight the lack of trust and political will among member nations, with India's dominant position and the enduring hostility between India and Pakistan being significant barriers.

Despite trying the historic-cultural affinity path to South Asian bonhomie, there are several persistent challenges that have caused the founding objectives of SAARC to still remain unrealised. Compared to other regional organisations, especially the EU or ASEAN, SAARC's record of achievements is not impressive. Some of the roadblocks to effective and efficient regional cooperation in South Asia are highlighted in the next section:

Challenges in SAARC

1. Rather than emerging from the people and their understanding of the cross-border civilisational unity of the region, SAARC was based on the nation-state formula of seven (later, eight) governments deciding to cooperate (Dixit, 2014).
2. The bureaucratic hindrances, mutual trust deficit, and the actual and perceived threats are big barriers, which kept South Asian countries from deeper intraregional trade connectivity (Kumar, 2020).
3. Despite high ambitions, the progress of SAARC has not been encouraging. The protracted conflict between India and Pakistan is one of the major obstacles to regional cooperation in South Asia. India has significant and legitimate complaints against its north-western neighbour, whose actions have also proven to be detrimental to regionalism. Pakistan's repeated use of non-state actors to attack India is a case in point. Pakistan views India as the inhibitor of SAARC's success, pointing to the hypothetical notion of Indian hegemony in the region (Muzaffar et al., 2017), to which it subscribes.
4. The stated novel objectives of SAARC, formed in 1985, began to take a backseat as its member states, namely, Afghanistan, Bangladesh, Bhutan, India, the Maldives, Nepal, Pakistan, and Sri Lanka, became engrossed in their domestic socio-economic and political development goals, complemented by trust deficit and occasional territorial disputes (Trigunayat, 2017).
5. Regionalism in South Asia also hinges upon bilateral relationships of India with its other smaller neighbours. For instance, intricate disputes, such as India's intervention in Sri Lanka and the Maldives, a regime-centric relationship with Bangladesh, and continued political conflict with Nepal, among numerous others, have created

a fractured geopolitical landscape marked by mistrust, suspicion, and intertwined inter-state conflicts (Huda and McDonald, 2016).

6. The slow progress of SAARC in the first decade of its existence, mainly due to the fact that India and Pakistan have remained mired in protracted conflicts, makes it imperative to foster new efforts. Commercial and economic linkages need to be better implemented for the benefit of the population in the region and catalyse regional understanding. However, the ambition that any project or activity must include all the member states of SAARC would be far from attainable. Hence, it must be avoided, where need be (Dixit, 2014).

While SAARC member states may have been able to cooperate on a few projects, the idea of regional integration has not been achieved yet in South Asia. Since its inception, the organisation has been unable to achieve any significant cooperation on matters relating to economy, transport and transit, or energy exchanges. The inability to realise an integrated regional economy has arisen due to how:

a) a. SAARC, as an organisation, has been structured;
b) . the political leadership has approached the conceptualisation of regionalism; and
c) c. the identities which have shaped the South Asian region.

SAARC, as an institution, and the principles on which it operates have been subject to harsh criticism. The clause of 'unanimity' enshrined in the SAARC Charter[1] has ensured that any country would have the ability to veto a decision. This power can be exercised irrespective of the needs and choices of other countries. For example, Pakistan refused to endorse the SAARC Regional Agreement on Railways and Regulation of Passenger and Cargo Vehicular Traffic amongst member states at the 18th SAARC summit. The multimodal transport agreement was to help facilitate the movement of cargo within the region. Such initiation would have helped India reach out to landlocked Afghanistan—the reason behind the reluctance of Pakistan.

Apart from the institutional design that has prevented the organisation from taking concrete actions, scholars like Kanak Mani Dixit (2014) have pointed fingers at the approach adopted by the respective member states that have prevented the optimisation of SAARC.

SAARC, as an organisation, did not originate from the wishes of the people of the region. Instead, the organisation is built in a bureaucratic, top-down approach. The key elements that should inform an organisation, namely, people-to-people contacts and civil society linkages, are missing (Dixit, 2014). Unfortunately, the concept of regionalism in South Asia has "not yet assumed a material reality of its own" (Yhome and Maini, 2017). The most probable reason behind the lack of a regional 'South Asian' identity could be the political and historical ties that bind the countries. Given the enormity of India—economically, militarily, and geographically—the smaller neighbouring states are bound to view it sceptically.

Inadequate support and lack of figures and spokespersons capable of commanding respect and building consensus in the South Asian region have hurt regional integration prospects (Huda and McDonald, 2016). Further, political rhetoric has not helped ease India's relations with her neighbours. The idea of the nation-state that gripped the region in the aftermath of colonialism has perpetrated an identity of differences. Such politically constructed differentiation has prevented the citizens of the South Asian countries from imagining their identities beyond the borders of their nations.

While the above description of challenges points towards the prevailing state in South Asia, it does not underestimate the enormous potential that the SAARC countries are endowed with, through their natural resources and geographic diversity (Muzaffar et al., 2017). However, while the South Asian countries are richly endowed with natural resources, especially energy resources, yet limited cooperation between them has increased the costs of energy requirements for each of them, thereby leading to insecurity in energy in the region as a whole.

India was a firm advocate of closer cooperation under Article VII, as it allowed member states to engage with each other in sub-regional cooperation. Article VII thus proved to be instrumental in moving away from the idea of a South Asian regional cooperation that was often met with roadblocks to the idea of a sub-regional cooperation, which was more practical and had the potential to become more successful in a shorter span of time. The section below discusses the origins of sub-regional cooperation in South Asia.

A Sub-Regional Framework for Cooperation in South Asia

With several impediments experienced already within the first decade of the establishment of SAARC and recognising the enormous potential for cooperation among countries willing to cooperate, in September 1996, India's then External Affairs Minister, Inder Kumar Gujral, in a lecture delivered at London's Royal Institute of International Affairs (RIIA), spoke about Bangladesh, India, Bhutan, and Nepal forming 'a dynamic area of growth' and reaffirmed the idea of sub-regional cooperation in the region.

The dynamic area of growth would mean that the huge growth potentials of the above four countries taken together, endowed with abundant human and natural resources, particularly gas, oil, coal, and water, if properly harnessed, would bring about collective prosperity for all. The requisite political will and policy coordination among the four countries, along with necessary communication infrastructure development, would herald growth and development and also promote trade and cultural linkages in the sub-region (Nuruzzaman, 1999).

At the 17th SAARC Council of Ministers' Meeting held in New Delhi from 19-20 December 1996, then Foreign Minister of Bangladesh, Abdus Samad Azad, formally floated the concept of sub-regional cooperation. Bangladesh and Nepal, through their Concept Paper on Sub-regional Cooperation in South Asia and Approach Paper for Sub-regional cooperation in SAARC, respectively, proposed for the initiation of sub-regional cooperation among Bangladesh, Bhutan, India (with a focus on its north-eastern states), and Nepal (BBIN). For Bangladesh, the objectives for sub-regional cooperation in South Asia included the exploitation of complementarities in resource endowment and comparative advantages through cross-border trade and investment flows in a contiguous zone of geographic unity. This sub-regional initiative was envisioned as an alternative way to promote economic collaboration, trade, and connectivity among the four nations (Pal, 2016), as they share similar socio-economic characteristics of a developing sub-region. For instance, they face similar energy problems like ever-growing energy demands vis-à-vis increased dependency on oil and gas imports and limited self-sufficiency in production from their indigenous sources; the dominance of single and traditional fuel in their domestic energy mix; lack of investment for energy infrastructure; and limited access to modern energy sources to a large portion of the population (Rahman et al., 2012; Government of India, 2020; Srivastava and Misra, 2007; Singh, 2013; Rahman et al., 2012). According to the World Bank, an electricity market of the BBIN countries—Bangladesh, Bhutan, India, and Nepal—would save an estimated $17 billion in capital costs and expand clean energy and hydropower capacity threefold by 2040 (World Bank, 2021).

There is a wide variation in the energy resource endowments among the countries, especially hydropower, natural gas, and coal resources. Nepal and Bhutan have huge hydropower potential but remain underutilised (Alam et al., 2017a; Lean and Smyth, 2014); coal is abundant in the eastern part of India (Ministry of Coal, Government of India, 2018); whereas reserves of natural gas are found in Bangladesh (Ministry of Power Energy and Mineral Resources, Bangladesh, 2019). Also, this sub-region is well endowed with renewable energy sources, such as solar, wind, and biomass, meeting a large portion of household energy demand across the region (Shukla, Sudhakar, and Baredar, 2017). Nepal and Bhutan, being land-locked countries with no significant fossil fuel reserves and production, rely totally on India for their fuel supply. The nature of available resources, seasonal characteristics of electricity demand and hydropower generation, geographical proximity, and willingness of sub-regional political regimes provide a notable opportunity, both in power trading and fossil fuel supply, within this sub-region. Thus, the utilisation of mutual economic complementarities on the basis of comparative advantage, for instance, immense water resources, development of hydropower and energy, promotion of trade and investment, expansion of telecommunication network, improvement of infrastructure of sustained economic development, and development of tourism industry, would truly make the sub-region a dynamic area of growth (Nuruzzaman, 1999).

Further, there are occasions in international relations when strengthening of bilateral ties leads to greater understanding between countries in geographical proximity. This happened in the case of India and Bangladesh, when the 1996 Ganges Treaty paved the way for strengthening economic ties with other countries of the subcontinent. Dhaka's push for the creation of a subregional group, consisting of Bangladesh, Bhutan, Nepal, and the north-eastern states of India, was warmly welcomed by India (Hossain, 1997). Toward that end, the foreign secretaries of India, Bangladesh, Nepal, and Bhutan met in Kathmandu on 2 April 1997. There the idea of a sub-regional grouping among the four countries received a gentle nudge forward. The meeting approved the idea of forming a quadrilateral economic cooperative framework of the SAARC. At the suggestion of Nepal, the new group was named as the South Asia Growth Quadrangle (SAGQ). The SAGQ announced its seven-point objectives and principles. It aimed at creating an environment for rapid economic development through identification and implementation of specific projects of cooperation in core economic sectors: multimodal transportation and communications, energy, trade and investment facilitation and promotion, tourism, and the optimal and sustainable use of natural resources (Hossain, 1998). The countries decided to adopt a project-led strategy to work together on commerce, communication, investment, energy, tourism, and the development of natural resources (Hassan, 2016).

The Asian Development Bank (ADB) launched the South Asian Sub-Regional Economic Cooperation (SASEC) programme that supported the SAGQ with regional technical assistance (RETA) projects (Ibid.). The rationale behind the ADB's support was that if the sub-region succeeds in fully achieving its potential, it would bring prosperity and a vastly improved quality of life for millions of people. Under the SASEC, the ADB provided financial and technical support to improve transport and energy connectivity, strengthen institutions and trade links, and boost human capital and capacity throughout the region (Asian Development Bank, 2005).

Under SASEC, from 2001-2013, more than $530 million worth of investments were made to develop necessary energy infrastructure and intra-regional power trade. For example, Bhutan's Green Power Development Project was to harness the power of water and the sun to provide electricity both to remote communities in Bhutan and to India. The development of renewable energy resources under the project continues to ensure the provision of power in an environmentally-friendly and sustainable manner. The Dagachhu hydropower sub-component produces 114 megawatts (MW) of power to be exported to India through an existing grid, implemented through a public-private partnership between Bhutan's public-sector Druk Green Power Corporation and India's Tata Power Company. The project harnesses solar power to provide electricity to schools, health centres, and other community facilities in remote mountain villages in Bhutan. ADB-financed energy projects in Nepal—where electricity supply is subject to long periods of scheduled outages and frequent unscheduled interruptions—are working to improve efficiency in the power sector, making power supply more reliable, and expand the country's transmission infrastructure to strengthen its capacity for cross-border energy trade. Together with energy infrastructure improvement and a focus on "green growth" in renewable energy options, the ADB supports the development of intra-regional SASEC power trade (Asian Development Bank, 2013).

The Bangladesh-India Electrical Grid Interconnection Project, under SASEC, has enabled the exchange of electricity through South Asia's first high-voltage direct current cross-border transmission link. It provides a 400-kilovolt double circuit transmission line between the electrical substations at Baharampur, India, and Bheramara, Bangladesh, reducing energy shortages in Bangladesh, providing an alternate market for Indian suppliers and improving grid stability in the region (Asian Development Bank, 2013).

However, despite the advancements made in BBIN sub-regional cooperation, the spirit of SAARC cooperation met with Pakistan's refusal to endorse the SAARC Regional Agreement on Railways and Regulation of Passenger and Cargo Vehicular Traffic in South Asia (Haran, 2018a). This demonstrated how political considerations took precedence over productive, forward-looking exchanges (Chaudhury et al., 2015).

Hence, at this time, the four countries of SAGQ rolled up their sleeves to foster sub-regionalism. This setback became a setup to revitalise the sub-regional initiatives as part of efforts to enhance regional connectivity. The persistent failure of living regional instruments to bring about significant change in trade, power, and infrastructural relations provided the motivation to gradually develop a consensus regarding sub-regional ties among four eastern neighbours of South Asia that extend beyond bilateral agreements.

The visit of Indian Prime Minister Narendra Modi to Bangladesh, Bhutan, and Nepal in 2014 marked a significant effort to bring the four countries to the negotiation table to advance sub-regional cooperation to new heights (Ministry of External Affairs, Government of India, 2014; Yhome, 2017). In his remarks at the 18th SAARC Summit in

Kathmandu, Modi discussed the increase in engagement between the four nations: "South Asia is slowly coming together. India and Bangladesh have strengthened their rail, road, electricity, and transit linkages. India and Nepal have begun a new era of energy cooperation, while India and Bhutan strengthen these connections." He also stated that regional integration in South Asia would go ahead "through SAARC or outside it, among all of us or some of us" (Modi, 2014).

The transport ministers of four countries—Minister for Physical Infrastructure and Transport of Nepal Bimalendra Nidhi, Minister of Road Transport and Bridges of Bangladesh Obaidul Quader, Bhutanese Minister for Information and Communications D.N. Dhungel, and Indian Minister for Road Transport and Highways and Shipping Nitin Gadkari—signed the landmark BBIN-MVA agreement on June 15, 2015, in Thimphu, with an intent to provide seamless people-to-people contact and enhance economic interaction by facilitating cross- border movement of people and goods between the BBIN countries (Ministry of External Affairs, 2015).

The BBIN vision for the sub-region rests on four mighty pillars: (i) trade connectivity and transit, (ii) investment in power generation and water management sectors, (iii) cooperation in the energy sector, including power trade and converting national grids into a sub-regional grid, and (iv) people-to-people connectivity. The primary objectives of the MVA, as noted in the Joint Declaration issued by the transport ministers of the BBIN countries, are as follows:

a. To facilitate cargo movement across sub-regional borders and significantly reduce trade transaction costs
b. To provide seamless people-to-people contact
c. To enhance economic integration by facilitating cross-border movement of people and goods
d. To facilitate cargo vehicle movement, as no change would be required at the borders

e. To establish a platform for these member nations to act decisively and implement collectively
f. To promote safe, cost-effective, and environmentally sound road transport in the sub-region and to further assist other member countries in creating an institutional mechanism for subregional integration (Ministry of External Affairs, Government of India, 2015a)

With a basic concept of a four- nation sub-regional framework in South Asia in place, it becomes important to understand the need for energy cooperation among the countries and then study the status of energy composition and utilisation and underutilisation of the energy resources of each country. The next section discusses this aspect.

Energy Cooperation in International Relations

International energy cooperation must be viewed in a wider perspective of political and economic stability and growth, besides the obvious and the most important goal of realising energy security. Energy cooperation among nations promotes economic growth through trade and helps unleash the tremendous potential of the partners involved (ADB, 2013). Energy cooperation among the member countries of a regional/sub-regional organisation has the potential to reduce import dependence, helping the region deal with power deficits and make it self-sufficient in energy. With enhanced access to electricity, fuel, and clean energy, the region will have higher growth rates and thereby enable billions of people to enhance their standard of living (Bhattacharjee, 2019).

The idea of energy security arose in the backdrop of the Gulf War of 1973-74, wherein the oil-exporting nations imposed an embargo on oil supplies. As a response to the weaponisation of oil, several industrialised countries came up with support policies to prevent such further events.

This led to the creation of the International Energy Agency (IEA), which called for setting up a collective action mechanism to respond effectively to potential disruptions in oil supply. Eventually, the IEA became the main international forum for energy cooperation on a variety of issues, such as security of supply, long-term policy, information transparency, energy efficiency, sustainability, research and development, technology collaboration, and international energy relations (IEA, 2023).

Traditionally, energy security has focused on oil and gas supply security and price stability and created a set of international energy governance regimes. Today, some of the trends that are reshaping the nature and focus of international energy cooperation and governance include the recognition by most governments and companies that energy security must be delivered alongside rapid action to reduce greenhouse gas (GHG) emissions and challenges of air pollution at the national level, and policy encouragement of cleaner energy options has helped spark technological advances and declining prices (Jigang and Webb, 2020). Further, energy security no longer relies specifically on ensuring a safe and smooth flow of supplies from producer countries. The scope of energy security has expanded to cover the entire chain of energy ranging from production till it reaches the consumers. This is primarily because energy infrastructures, such as oil and gas pipelines and high-transmission voltage lines and their management systems, are all prone to disruptions. In other words, the concept of cooperative energy security merges international environmental and energy concerns, focusing on sustainable development. The energy industry's current success is due to the new phenomenon of strategic alliances among industry leaders, addressing complex engineering tasks that blend economic, political, and social elements. This idea of a "strategic alliance" also applies politically to the traditional relationship between civil society and government in democratic theory. Hence, today's necessity is not a "public-private partnership" but a three-way strategic alliance involving governments, industry, and the citizens (Cutler, 2007).

The broader policy interests that are linked to energy governance and cooperation, from economic performance to ensuring basic amenities, are inextricably linked to domestic energy choices—regardless of a country being dependent on energy imports or it being an energy exporter. To achieve these strategic policy interests, governments will need to use a combination of bilateral and multilateral approaches to manage these choices effectively. In essence, cooperation is important to effectively implement an integrated and efficient approach to energy cooperation that will support the attainment of Sustainable Development Goals, including a resilient recovery from the COVID-19 pandemic. Multi-stakeholder and multilateral efforts are needed to accelerate progress towards practical integrated water and energy solutions. Countries may consider rewards and support for innovative solutions, especially from the private sector and start-ups, providing a transformative path, resulting in energy security and ensuring that no one is left behind.

The section below shows the composition of energy resources of the BBIN countries. Within the framework of SDG and the policy choices of each country to reduce carbon emissions, this section discusses the Nationally Determined Contributions (NDCs) and understands their renewable energy (RE) potential. Given the RE potential, the section then discusses the significance of energy cooperation amongst the BBIN countries to ensure energy security in the sub-region and a win-win situation for all.

Energy Composition

The BBIN sub-region is one of the leading consumers of energy, and hydrocarbon accounts for a predominant share of its energy mix. The countries are neither richly endowed with hydrocarbons nor evenly bestowed with natural resources and production capabilities. Coal accounts for about 41.9 per cent of the total primary energy supply of the BBIN sub-region, mainly because of the operation of coal-fired power plants to generate electricity and use of coking coal in the steel industry, particularly in India, which is home to 87 per cent of the total population but responsible for 94 per cent of primary energy requirements of this sub-region (Garg et al., 2017; Gyanwali et al., 2020). India's dependency on coal for energy production is evident from the fact that about 66 per cent of India's energy needs are met by the country's thermal power plants, with 53 per cent of that total coming from coal (Kumar and Prasad, 2023). India imports a large amount of crude oil and exports refined products to Nepal, Bhutan, Bangladesh, and other countries (Wijayatunga and Fernando, 2013; Kumar et al., 2023). Natural gas contributed to a small share of the energy mix in India (about 5.7 per cent) and is negligible in Nepal and Bhutan but very high in Bangladesh (about 57 per cent) in 2017. It is mainly used in power plants and the fertiliser industry and has a growing role in the residential sector and as a transportation fuel. The role of hydropower in Bhutan and Nepal is dominant in electricity generation, and owing to decrement in technology cost and clean energy initiatives, the share of solar PV and wind is increasing.

Overall, limited domestic production of petroleum products and gas in this sub-region has led to a highly increased dependency on imported fossil energy. A consequence of the growing economies of BBIN has been the creation of a structural environment of a regional deficit in energy. There is an imbalance between the demand for energy and supply from local sources, which results in increased import dependence. Table 1.1 shows this clearly. According to the latest available data, the World Bank reported that the import dependence varies from about 25 per cent in the case of Bhutan to about 17 per cent in the case of Nepal. In the case of larger countries like India and Bangladesh, it is more than 80 per cent of their hydrocarbon demand (The World Bank, 2019).

Table 1.1: Energy Indicators in BBIN Countries

	Total energy supply	Energy use (TES) per capita	Energy intensity	Self-sufficiency	Renewable share in TFEC	Electricity consumption per capita
	PJ	GJ	MJ/INTL $	per cent	per cent	kWh
Bangladesh	1,963.5	12.2	2.7	81.6	39.7	436.3
Bhutan	70.9	94	8.3	108.2	81.1	2,897.3
India	39,184.3	29	4.5	60.9	27.2	856.3
Nepal	592.9	21.1	6.5	75.3	76.4	231.5
Notes: PJ: Petajoules; GJ: Gigajoules; TES: Total Energy Supply; MJ: Megajoules; TFEC: Total Final Electricity Consumption Source: 2021 Energy Statistics Pocketbook, United Nations Statistics Division, https://unstats.un.org/unsd/energystats/pubs/documents/2021pb-web.pdf						

Source: Energy Efficiency in South Asia, Asian Development Bank Report, December 2021, https://www.adb.org/sites/default/files/publication/761251/energy-efficiency-south-asia-opportunities.pdf

Fossil fuel deposits in this sub-region are mainly available in India and Bangladesh whereas Bhutan and Nepal do not have significant fossil fuel deposits. As per the latest data available, in 2023, India ranked second in coal and lignite production with 1045 Metric Tonnes (Mt), next to China with 4075 Mt (Enerdata, 2024). According to the 2022 report of the Geological Survey of India, the coal inventory was 361411.46 million tonnes (*Press Information Bureau*, 2023a). Coal resources in India are largely concentrated in the states of Jharkhand (28 per cent), Odisha (22 per cent), Chhattisgarh (15 per cent), and West Bengal (9 per cent) with the remainder being lignite (Ministry of Coal, Government of India, 2018; Kumar and Prasad, 2023; Ministry of Coal, Government of India, 2024).

The five major coalfields of Bangladesh are located in Jamalganj, Barapukuria, Khalashpur, Digipara, and Phulbari (Uddin, 2022). These coal basins are located in the north-western part of Bangladesh and contain high-volatile, low-sulphur bituminous coal, with total reserves exceeding three billion tonnes (Ibid.).

In India, crude oil reserves stood at 651.77 million tonnes in 2022 against 591.92 million tonnes in 2021. The geographical distribution of crude oil indicates that the maximum reserves are in the Western Offshore (33 per cent) followed by Assam (23 per cent). The reserves of natural gas in 2022 were estimated at 1138.67 billion cubic metres, and the maximum reserves of natural gas are located in the Western Offshore (29.6 per cent) followed by Eastern offshore (23.6 per cent) (Ministry of Statistics and Programme Implementation, Government of India, 2023).

The BBIN sub-region has abundant potential for solar photovoltaic (PV) installation, assuming the utilisation of wasteland and rooftop solar panels, making it the most secure resource from a clean energy security perspective. For instance, in Bangladesh, the solar energy installed capacity in terms of on-grid and off-grid technology till 2020 was 333.66 MW and 83.02 MW, respectively, making a total of 416. 68 MW (Podder et al., 2021). Bhutan's Alternative Energy Policy 2013 formulated specific targets for electricity generation of 5 MW each from solar, wind, and biomass and energy generation of 3 MW equivalent each from biomass and solar thermal (Malla and Dhananjayan, 2023). Very recently, in 2021, a 180kW grid-tied ground mounted solar photo-voltaic power plant was commissioned and inaugurated. It marked the beginning of Bhutan's investment in grid-tied solar energy as a viable alternative energy source in the face of soaring domestic demand and climate change. The solar plant, co-located with the existing 600 kW wind farm at Rubesa, is expected to generate 263,000 units of energy a year, which will be adequate for supplying electricity to around 80-90 households (United Nations Development Programme, 2021). The Bhutanese government is committed to complete the country's first large solar plant, the 17 MW project in Sephu, Wangduephodrang, by mid-2025, and plans to harness 300 MW of solar energy as it seeks to diversify its grid (Gyeltshen, 2022). The total installed capacity of solar energy in India is 84.27 GW (*Invest India*, 2024). Nepal possesses vast solar resources, and there has been increasing policy interest in the use of solar PV systems. About 1.1 million solar home systems, rated at nearly 30 Megawatt-peak (MWp)[2], have been installed across Nepal (Kafle et al., 2023).

The total installed capacity of wind energy in India is 46.42 GW (*Invest India*, 2024). The Government of India is fully committed to achieve the target of 500 GW renewable energy capacity by the year 2030 (*Press Information Bureau*, 2023b).

In Bangladesh, three wind farms with a total power output of 2.9 MW have already been installed and are operating at Kutubdia (Cox's Bazar) and Sonagazi (Feni); two additional plants with a capacity of 62 MW are currently undergoing construction at Chakaria (Cox's Bazar) and Sirajganj Sadar; and three additional plants with a capacity of 295 MW are in the planning stages at Kalapara (Patuakhali), Chandpur Sadar (Cox's Bazar, Mongla, Sonagazi-2), and Maheshkhali (Cox's Bazar) (Abdullah-Al-Mahbub and Islam, 2024).

Clearly, the complementarities in the energy demand, vulnerability to fluctuations in the global market, uneven resource endowments, and increasing challenges posed by global warming and climate change underscore the need to cooperate and achieve regional energy security. The section below discusses the voluntary commitments made by the BBIN nations as their pledge to reduce greenhouse gas emissions and adapt to the impacts of climate change. One way towards adapting and mitigating the impacts is investing in renewable energy. Known as Nationally Determined Contributions (NDCs), these commitments are discussed below, which will be followed by a discussion on the RE potential of the BBIN countries.

Nationally Determined Contribution Targets of the BBIN Countries

Bangladesh

Bangladesh has committed that by the year 2030, 100 per cent coal power plants will be using ultra supercritical technology; efficient running of vehicles will lead to 15 per cent improvement in efficiency of vehicles; there would be a 10 per cent energy consumption reduction in the industry sector compared to business as usual by 2030 and 70 per cent and 20 per cent market share of improved biomass cook stoves and improved gas stoves, respectively; improved and enhanced Inland Water Transport (IWT) system (improve navigation for regional, sub-regional, and local routes, improve maintenance of water vessels to enhance engine performance, introduce electric water vessels etc.); implementation of renewable energy projects of 911.8 MW, with the following components: Grid-connected Solar-581 MW, Wind-149 MW, Biomass-20 MW, Biogas-5 MW, New Hydro-100 MW, Solar Mini-grid-56.8 MW; installation of new Combined Cycle Gas- based power plant (3208 MW); efficiency improvement of existing gas turbine power plant (570 MW); and installation of prepaid metres across the country. Overall, the country has committed to a reduction in the energy consumption of the commercial sector by 25 per cent compared to business as usual.

The Mujib Climate Prosperity Plan up to 2030, launched in 2020, seeks to provide a strategic investment framework to mobilise financing, especially through international cooperation, for implementing renewable energy and climate resilience initiatives. The draft plan identified several key initiatives, which focus on renewable energy, energy storage infrastructure, power grid modernisation, established carbon market regime, Bangladesh Delta Plan 2100 resilience bonds, training and skills development for future, future-proof Bangladesh's industries, locally-led adaptation outcomes, micro, small and medium enterprise (MSME) financial protection and productivity enhancement, climate-resilient and nature-based agricultural and fisheries development, environment friendly transport, climate resilient well-being programmes and accelerated digital revolution. The National Solar Energy Roadmap, 2021–2041 has been drafted to frame a long-term vision for the nation and set possible capacity targets for the country's solar energy initiative. Towards this, the cost of key mitigation measures in energy from 2021–2030 is estimated at USD 1,39,456.30 million (Ministry of Environment, Forests and Climate Change, Government of Bangladesh, 2021).

Bhutan

The Kingdom of Bhutan made the commitment to remain carbon neutral in 2009 despite being a small, mountainous developing country with many other pressing social and economic development needs and priorities. This commitment was made with the view that there is no need greater, or more important, than keeping the planet safe for life to continue. Bhutan's Intended Nationally Determined Contribution (INDC) has reiterated the country's resolve to remain carbon neutral by ensuring that its emission of GHGs does not exceed the sink capacity of its forests. For this, it is committed to improving efficiency in freight transport and existing vehicles through standards and capacity building; promoting non-fossil fuel-powered and non-motorised transport, such as fuel cell and electric vehicles; improvement of manufacturing processes and technologies in existing industries; and promoting energy efficiency in appliances and buildings (National Environment Commission, 2015).

India

India has exhibited great agility in its commitments towards climate change adaptation and mitigation efforts. Its NDCs, as submitted to the United Nations Framework Convention on Climate Change (UNFCCC), seek to promote ultra-supercritical technology for coal power plants; promote energy efficiency in buildings, appliances, transport, and industry; promote the Zero Effect, Zero Defect with Make in India campaign to enhance energy and resource efficiency, pollution control, use of renewable energy, and waste management, etc.; promote faster adoption and manufacturing of hybrid and electric vehicles in the country by providing incentives under the National Electric Mobility Mission Plan 2020; and improve fuel standards by switching from Bharat Stage IV fuels to Bharat Stages V and VI across the country in the near future. It has also committed to achieve about 50 per cent cumulative electric power installed capacity from non-fossil fuel-based energy resources by 2030, with the help of transfer of technology and low-cost international finance, including from Green Climate Fund (GCF) (Government of India, 2022).

Nepal

Government of Nepal's enhanced Nationally Determined Contribution (NDC), under the Paris Agreement for the period 2021–2030, seeks to promote clean energy and energy-efficient technology; have a 20 per cent increment in the share of electric vehicles by 2020 compared to 2010 vehicle stock; promote public transport systems and bicycle use; and increase improved cooking stoves by around 475,000 stoves to improve energy efficiency in cooking. Further, it seeks to expand clean energy generation from approximately 1,400 MW to 15,000 MW, of which 5-10 per cent will be generated from mini and micro-hydro power, solar, wind and bio-energy by 2030. Of this, 5,000 MW is an unconditional target. The remainder is dependent upon the provision of funding by the international community. Nepal is also committed to ensure that 15 per cent of the total energy demand is supplied from clean energy sources (Government of Nepal, 2020).

Renewable Energy Endowments in BBIN

There is a wide variation in commercial energy resource endowments and commercial energy demand among the BBIN countries. While India and Bangladesh account for the major natural gas and coal resources, Bhutan and Nepal have large hydropower resources. All the countries have vast renewable energy potential, and the sharing of these resources naturally leads to more optimal energy supply solutions for the entire sub-region. The sub-region, however, needs enhanced regional energy transfer to leverage economies of scale through a more vibrant intra- and inter-regional energy trade structure (Wijayatunga and Fernando, 2013). As discussed in the previous sections, domestic and sub-regional energy resources in the sub-region have not been fully exploited, and shortages have caused an increasing dependence on fuel imports from outside the region (SASEC, 2013).

Of late, out of growing concerns of climate change and environmental degradation, BBIN countries have begun to place an emphasis on reducing their overdependence on fossil fuels while simultaneously managing the growing demand for energy. Thus, an alternative energy option, that is renewable energy (RE), has gained prominence for the nations. Some of the advantages of various types of renewable energy are:

Solar Energy: It is used for cooking, lighting, and water heating and requires less consumption of fuel wood, kerosene, and batteries, leading to improved local air quality. The adaptation benefits include rural electrification and access to information and communication technology, and the socio-economic benefits include improved quality of life as well as better health and sanitation through streetlights and boiled water. Solar power is a rapidly developing industry in India. The Indian government put forward ambitious solar plans in January 2015, targeting 100 GW of solar capacity (including 40 GW from rooftop solar) by 2022 with an investment of about 100 billion USD. The National Action Plan on Climate Change (NAPCC), released by the Government of India in

2008, set eight national missions to focus on promoting understanding of climate change, adaptation and mitigation, energy efficiency, and natural resource conservation (*Press Information Bureau*, 2021). One of the missions was the National Solar Mission, which was launched in 2010. The initial target of NSM was to install 20 GW solar power by 2022. This was upscaled to 100 GW in early 2015. Numerous facilitative programmes and schemes under the mission drove the grid- connected solar power installed capacity from 25 MW in the year 2010-11 to about 36.32 GW as on October 31, 2020 (Ibid.). This was also facilitated by the International Solar Alliance (ISA) that was co-founded by India along with France on the sidelines of the 21st Conference of Parties (COP21) to the United Nations Framework Convention on Climate Change (UNFCCC) held in Paris in November 2025. The ISA intended to promote solar energy in the sunshine belt of countries, mostly between the Tropic of Cancer and the Tropic of Capricorn (International Solar Alliance, 2024). The latest data as per *Invest India* shows that the total installed capacity in solar energy in India is 84.27 GW by 2024. India has also been promoting solar pump programmes to support farmers, and it is one of the initiatives taken by the Indian government to introduce solar energy in agriculture (Shidore and Busby, 2019).

Bangladesh has also set RE development targets of installing an additional 3.1 GW capacity by 2021, mostly from solar, along with wind and biomass. However, the implementation of the same has been slow (Sustainable and Renewable Energy Development Authority, 2015; Hil Baky, Rahman, and Islam, 2017; Hossain, Hossain, and Uddin, 2017). Till 2018, there were no grid-connected solar parks or solar rooftops in Bangladesh, but solar parks with a total installed capacity of about 45 MW were under construction, and about 14 MW off-grid solar rooftop PV and 150 MW solar home systems were installed (Marzia et al., 2018; Sharif et al., 2018). Till 2020, the solar energy installed capacity in terms of on-grid and off-grid technology till 2020 was 333.66 MW and 83.02 MW, respectively, making it a total of 416.68 MW (Podder et al., 2021).

Nepal is located at a latitude of 26–30°N and receives more than 300 days of sunlight per year. Nepal has a moderately high insolation of about 4.7 kWh/m^2 day (17 MJ/m^2 day) and receives an average of 6.8 hours of sunshine per day (Solar Electric Manufacturer's Association Nepal (SEMAN), 2019). This makes solar energy the most significant RE generation potential in the country. The first large size solar power plant of 25 MW in Nepal was commissioned in 2017 with financial support from the World Bank in Nuwakot district, near Kathmandu (Thapa, 2022). According to interviews conducted with experts in Kathmandu, on sunny days, the plant produces 100,000 units of electricity daily. The Department of Electricity Development of Nepal has approved survey licences for different locations with a cumulative capacity of about 320 MW.

Likewise, the government of Bhutan has also taken several initiatives for rural electrification through off-grid installation and conducting a feasibility study for the 30 MW Shingkhar solar project in Bumthang district with financial assistance from the Asian Development Bank.

Hydro Energy: Hydro energy, a renewable and low-carbon energy source, is crucial for achieving energy security and sustainability goals. The BBIN region, with its abundant water resources, rivers, and mountainous terrain, is ideal for hydropower development. Hydro energy projects enhance energy security in BBIN countries by reducing dependence on imported fossil fuels, thereby mitigating the effects of energy price fluctuations and supply disruptions.

Hydropower offers critical grid stability and flexibility, acting as a balancing power source. Unlike intermittent renewables like wind and solar, hydropower can quickly adjust to demand changes, making it invaluable for grid balancing. Its quick start capability and high peak load factor enable it to meet peak load demands instantly, ensuring reliable power during high demand periods. Environmentally safe and non-polluting, hydropower can also operate at zero loads. Additionally, pumped storage hydro plants store water during low-demand periods and release it to generate power during peak hours, effectively balancing supply and demand on the grid. This balancing capability is essential for a stable and resilient electricity grid, making hydropower indispensable. Moreover, hydropower projects preserve soil fertility by regulating sediment flow, which enhances agricultural productivity and replenishes groundwater discharge. Hydropower has also become a significant component of cross-border power trade in the BBIN region (Confederation of Indian Industries, 2023).

Hydropower is used for lighting and agricultural processing. It has the mitigation benefit of reduced greenhouse gases and protection of land and the adaptation benefit of improved social resilience with evident improved yield in the agricultural sector. Most of the hydro resources in this sub-region are perennial and originate from the high Himalayas, but the water flow rate is not consistent throughout the year and is also subject to seasonal variation, causing fluctuation in power generation during wet and dry seasons. Hydropower plants constructed with large dams can store water during the wet season and utilise it during the dry season but are associated with high environmental risks.

The hydropower potential of India is around 1,45,000 MW and at 60 per cent load factor, it can meet the demand of around 85,000 MW. Around 26 per cent of the potential has been exploited in India at around 42 GW (Ministry of Power, Government of India, 2024; *The Economic Times*, 2024). While a huge potential remains unharnessed, it also necessitates new long-distance transmission lines to transfer power to load centres from remotely located potential sites (Gopalakrishnan, 2015). Most of the potential sites are distributed in Arunachal Pradesh, Himachal Pradesh, Uttarakhand, and Jammu and Kashmir (Ministry of New and Renewable Energy, 2024a).

Apart from large hydro, the assessment of small hydro (2 MW to 25 MW) potential has indicated nearly 21 GW distributed over 7133 sites for power generation in the country from small/mini hydel projects. This was assessed by the Hydro and Renewable Energy Department (HRED), earlier known as the Alternate Hydro Energy Centre (AHEC) of IIT, Roorkee, and the data was compiled as Small Hydro Database of July 2016 (Ibid.). Hydropower projects of about 15 GW are at various stages of construction, and the Government of India aims to further develop capacity. It is poised to reach 67 GW by 2031-32 (*The Economic Times*, 2024).

Hydropower constitutes 3.5 per cent of Nepal's energy basket (Ministry of Finance, Government of Nepal), and almost 97 per cent of the electrical energy is obtained from hydropower (90 per cent run-of-the river (RoR) (Department of Electricity Development, Government of Nepal, 2021). The current installed hydro capacity of 149 projects is about 2736 MW (Department of Electricity Development, Government of Nepal, 2024). The theoretical potential of hydropower in the country is about 83,000 MW, of which roughly 42,000 MW are considered economically viable (USAID, 2018).

The electricity generation falls below 40 per cent during winter because almost 90 per cent of the existing hydropower projects are the ROR type (Department of Electricity Development, Government of Nepal, 2021). Most of the surface water in Nepal drains through four major rivers: the Saptakoshi, Narayani, Karnali, and Mahakali, and their tributaries originate either from the Himalayas or from the Tibetan Plateau (Jha, 2011). The huge hydropower resources remain untapped because Nepal neither has enough financial resources for investment nor technical human resources to explore their full potential (Adhikari, 2021). This is further exacerbated by land and environmental concerns caused by flooding at or near dam sites; the excessive dependence of the country on hydropower; and lack of a diversified energy mix (Lohani and Blakers, 2021). According to interviews conducted with experts, the Government of Nepal is seeking foreign and private investments to construct large hydro storage projects and is establishing power trade agreements with India and Bangladesh as potential markets for power sale.

Like Nepal, the power system of Bhutan is also hydropower-dominated. With an installed capacity of 1.6 GW, Bhutan has enormous hydropower potential, boasting over 35 GW of clean renewable energy from more than 150 sites nationwide and an annual production capability of 154,000 gigawatt hours (GWh) (Ministry of Economic Affairs, Royal Government of Bhutan, 2021). The country has so far developed just 7 per cent of its hydropower potential, yet the sector already accounts for an impressive 40 per cent of national revenue (Almulhem, 2023).

The majority of potential sites are concentrated in the Wangchhu, Punatsangchhu, Mangdechhu, and Drangmechhu river basins. All these rivers have large snow-fed perennial flows, hence afford attractive possibilities of hydro-electric development. The Government of Bhutan plans to develop its clean hydropower for fulfilling its domestic demand as well as to export the surplus power to neighbouring countries (Alam et al., 2017). However, the challenge facing the sector is the low proportion of power vis-a-vis the installed capacity as every hydropower project developed so far is a ROR scheme (Ministry of Economic Affairs, Royal Government of Bhutan, 2021).

The Sustainable Hydropower Development Policy 2008 of Bhutan was revised and came into effect from March 17, 2021. It intended to provide universal access to sustainable energy for alleviating poverty and boosting productivity; ensuring energy security for the economic development of the country by providing secure, adequate, reliable, and competitively priced electricity; enhancing cross- border trade of electricity by participating in the evolving and innovative market mechanisms; securing/mobilising funds for sustainable development of hydropower projects; developing hydropower in a regionally equitable manner to benefit all the people of Bhutan; ensuring optimal use of water resources through integration with other end uses and alternative energy resources; contributing towards development of clean energy and technologies to adapt and mitigate problems related to global warming and climate change; strengthening the institutional arrangements and national capacities in the hydropower sector; promoting hydropower-related "water to wire" and other energy storage businesses, such as hydrogen fuel, green ammonia, and other emerging technologies; creating an enabling ecosystem for participation and engagement of the Bhutanese citizens in the construction of hydropower projects, including providing goods and services; and promoting Research, Demonstration and Development (RD&D) and creating centres of excellence and knowledge hubs in the region for the entire value chain of hydropower, including hybrid energy technologies (Ibid.).

The ongoing 10 GW hydropower projects are being developed in bilateral cooperation with India in the framework of mutual trust. Building on the success of the 720 MW Mangdechhu Hydro-electric Project, Prime Minister Narendra Modi and Prime Minister Dasho Tshering Tobgay, on March 22, 2024, agreed to commission the 1020 MW Punatsangchhu-II Hydro-electric Project by the end of 2024. Both sides welcomed the positive expert-level discussions on a technically sound and cost-effective way forward for 1200 MW Punatsangchhu – I HEP (Modi, 2024).

Hydropower in Bangladesh has limited potential due to concerns about land use and flooding and the absence of high head and flow rates (Hussain et al., 2019; Us Salehin, 2024). As of 2022, Bangladesh maintains a consistent hydropower capacity of 230 MW from Kaptai Hydroelectric plant, established in 1962, which is the only storage-based hydropower station under operation in Bangladesh (Us Salehin, 2024).

Wind Energy: It is used for power generation, crop processing, irrigation, and water pumping. The mitigation benefits include decreased dependence on wood/biogas and avoidance of carbon dioxide (CO_2) emissions while the adaptation benefits include reduced vulnerability to water scarcity and more adaptation choices through irrigated agriculture. The socio-economic development benefits include income generation, improved quality of life, reduced risks of vector- borne diseases, improved water supply/food security, school attendance (especially for girls), and reduced migration.

Due to its advanced and reasonably priced energy conversion turbine technology, wind energy is today considered one of the most important, rapidly expanding, widely used, and financially appealing renewable energy sources for producing electrical energy (Chandel and Anjum, 2013; Hasan et al., 2024).

Though the government of Bangladesh plans for developing 1.37 GW wind power by 2021; due to limited potential, a 900 kilowatts (kW) plant at the Muhuri Dam and a 1 MW plant on Kutubdia remain the only grid-connected wind farms currently operating in the country. Research has shown that the locations with the highest average wind speeds include Sandwip, Patuakhali, Subarnachar, Noakhali, Charfasson, Bhola, and Barisal. Sandwip, an island located along the south-eastern coast of Bangladesh in the Chittagong District, was the best site in Bangladesh for wind energy production with the average wind speed value of 4.89 metre per second. The greatest Sandwip yearly speed ever recorded was 5.18 metre per second in 2017 (Hasan, 2024).

However, the issues related to land acquisition, grids, and financing in this sub-region create some hindrances, leading to a slower rate of deployment. Wind energy has become one of the most promising alternative energy technologies, particularly in the northern, southern, and western parts of India. There is also considerable potential for offshore wind power production. Tamil Nadu, Gujarat, Rajasthan, Andhra Pradesh, Maharashtra, Karnataka, Madhya Pradesh, and Telangana are significantly ahead in wind power production, making India the fourth largest country with 43.7 GW installed capacity, contributing about 4 per cent of total generated power, and with a target to achieve 60 GW by 2022. With the current pace, it is likely to increase to 99.9 GW by 2029-30 (World Institute of Sustainable Energy, Pune, 2017; *Press Information Bureau*, 2023c).

Nepal has relatively low wind potential and has limited investments in wind installations (Global Wind Atlas, 2020). Only the ridges of the high Himalayas are found to be favourable for wind energy. But the topographies are generally inaccessible to wind turbines, thereby rendering wind more expensive than other RE sources (Lohani et al., 2023). The potential of wind energy in Nepal and Bhutan is not yet fully explored due to the lack of real-time and historical wind data, and they also do not have any significant installed capacity. The Rubesa wind farm is an instance of Bhutan seeking to diversify its energy mix.

Bio-Power: It helps in electricity generation and heat, which has mitigation benefits like reduced use of charcoal and fuel wood and less pressure on natural resources. It helps in adaptation benefits like reduction in the likelihood of deforestation and desertification. It creates jobs and livelihood opportunities, reduces drudgery, and reduces incidents related to indoor air pollution and respiratory infections. Biogas is used as thermal energy and for production of sludge for fertilisers, which helps in reduction in the usage of charcoal, fuel wood, and liquefied petroleum gas and reduced use of pesticides and fertilisers. The adaptation benefits include reduction in the likelihood of deforestation, adapting to soil erosion, aridity, and reduced environmental degradation. The socio-economic development benefits include reduced drudgery, reduction of incidents related to respiratory infections, and better prospects for agricultural productivity and income generation (Shukla et al., 2017).

Biomass is advantageous over other forms of renewable energy due to its capacity for storage and easy year-round accessibility from diverse sources. Among renewable energy sources, biomass has the important characteristics of being almost carbon neutral and abundantly available from a range of sources (Kibria et al., 2024). Bio-power projects are largely distributed across India on a small scale with the installed capacity of about 10.23 GW as of March 2023, the majority of which is based on bagasse and a small portion on co-generation and gasification technologies (*Press Information Bureau*, 2023d). Most of the power plants based on bagasse, a by-product of sugarcane, are operated in Andhra Pradesh, Maharashtra, Karnataka, Uttar Pradesh, and Tamil Nadu, whereas other biomass-based power plants installed in rural areas use locally available rice husk, cotton stalks, and agro-residues to supply electricity for lighting and water pumping (*Press Information Bureau*, 2023d; Tripathi et al., 2016). However, lack of structured networks for collection, transportation, and storage of biomass and the comparatively high cost offer notable hindrances (Feng, 2022). Policy support from the government, for instance, SATAT (Sustainable Alternative Towards Affordable Transportation envisaged production of 15 MMT of compressed biogas from 5000 plants by 2023. The Ministry of New and Renewable Energy, Government of India, has encouraged farmers in rural areas to operate biomass-based power plants, using locally available resources (Ministry of New and Renewable Energy, 2024). The MNRE notified the National Bioenergy Programme from 2021-2026 with an outlay of Rs. 858 crore under Phase-I, which comprise the following sub-schemes:

1. Waste to Energy Programme (Programme on Energy from Urban, Industrial and Agricultural Wastes /Residues)
2. Biomass Programme (Scheme to Support Manufacturing of Briquettes & Pellets and Promotion of Biomass (non-bagasse) based cogeneration in Industries)
3. Biogas Programme (Ibid.; Ministry of New and Renewable Energy, 2022a).

Organic crop residues, animal waste, and municipal solid waste are the most accessible biomass energy sources in Bangladesh (Hasan et al., 2021). Currently, there is a 250 kW off-grid rice husk plant in

Kapasia, financed by Infrastructure Development Company Limited (IDCOL) at Tk. 2.50 crore (IDCOL, 2007). A 400 kW rice husk plant is proposed in Thakurgaon in Bangladesh (Power Division, Ministry of Power, Energy, and Mineral Resources, 2015). Bhutan and Nepal are also promoting biomass-based power generation, but the achievements are not remarkably significant.

Nuclear Power: India initiated its nuclear power programme nearly 60 years ago with the goal of optimally using its indigenous raw materials, i.e., limited uranium but large thorium reserves (Banerjee and Gupta, 2017). Though large deposits of uranium and thorium have been discovered in India, Russia still remains the major supplier of nuclear fuel.

As of March 2019, nuclear power is the fifth largest source of electricity in India, generated by seven nuclear power plants with 22 nuclear reactors with a total installed capacity of 6.78 GW. The existing nuclear power plants are located in Rajasthan, Uttar Pradesh, Gujarat, Maharashtra, Karnataka, and Tamil Nadu. India has a strong commitment to boost its nuclear capacity up to 23–34 GW to meet its increasing electricity demand and improve its energy security on a low-carbon basis (NITI Aayog, 2018; Mohan, 2016), but public concerns will play an important role in the prospects for nuclear power. Indian researchers are working to design and develop a prototype for an atomic reactor using thorium and plan to have a first pilot reactor in service by 2022 and commercial reactors deployed by around 2030.

Bangladesh committed to low carbon economic development and is constructing its first nuclear power plant in Rooppur with strong technical and financial support from the Russian state energy commission, with an expected generation of 2.4 GW of power by the year 2024 (Karim et al., 2018). The government is also exploring the feasibility of constructing the next nuclear plant, and several sites are under consideration (Ashraf and Islam, 2018). But countries like Nepal and Bhutan do not have any plan and policy to promote nuclear power.

The BBIN countries have inexhaustible and replenishable alternative energy sources potential, such as solar power, wind power, hydroelectricity, and biofuels. They have enormous potential to attract investment, provide energy security through diversification, spur technological research, and enhance stable economic growth (Shukla et al., 2017). They have begun to place an emphasis on reducing their overdependence on fossil fuels while simultaneously managing the growing demand for energy. This is at the core of the development of the sub-region. However, the energy sector is the sub-region's largest greenhouse gas emitter, contributing to air pollution, imposing a high burden of disease, and possibly stunting economic growth (Chen, 2022; Health Effects Institute, 2018). Therefore, the decarbonisation of the energy sector is instrumental to the region's sustainable growth. RE is key in the transition to green, secure, and affordable energy, as they can help countries build resilience to volatile prices, lower energy costs, and mitigate climate change. While South Asia has a huge renewable energy potential, Bhutan and Nepal are the only countries that rely on renewable sources as their primary energy source, although the latter still relies heavily on imported petroleum products for its transportation sector (World Bank Data, 2023). Others continue to use fossil fuels, although India's solar and wind market is rapidly developing (Triyana and Li, 2022; World Bank, 2021).

The potential for RE in the BBIN sub-region is wide-ranging. Bhutan and Nepal produce vast quantities of hydroelectric energy, and their capacity is increasing. India and Bangladesh can harness wind and solar potential, creating opportunities to replace existing coal-fired capacity with renewables. The climate of BBIN can be divided into three basic categories: tropical, dry, and temperate, which is favourable for a variety of renewable energy sources. A scenario that prioritises energy security through better energy efficiency involves switching to natural gas and higher shares of renewables. To utilise these potentials, the governments of BBIN have announced various programmes and policies encouraging industries and individuals to deploy renewable energy-powered systems in power applications. Unlike fossil fuels, renewables are more uniformly distributed across the region, and declining costs of renewables, along with the governments' policies on greenhouse gas (GHG) emission reduction and improved national energy security, have created a favourable situation for further capacity addition (Gyanwali et al., 2020).

The section below discusses the RE potential of each of the BBIN countries.

Renewable Energy Potential in the BBIN

Bhutan

Bhutan is geographically located between China and India and is a landlocked country. Hydropower is the single largest contributor to Bhutan's economy. Power exports constitute 45 per cent of the revenue of the Royal Government of Bhutan (RGoB) and 12 per cent of Bhutan's Gross Domestic Product (GDP) (The International Bank for Reconstruction and Development/The World Bank, 2008). Resources mobilised by harnessing Bhutan's hydropower potential through run-of-the-river (RoR) schemes, keeping in view the economic viability of these projects, are critical for future growth and diversification of the economy (World Bank, 2007).

Bhutan's hydropower potential is estimated at over 30,000 MW, of which it is commercially and technologically feasible to tap 23760 MW. Less than 10 per cent of this has been tapped so far (Haran, 2022). The existing hydro projects have been developed with foreign aid, primarily from India (three projects) and Austria (two projects). The addition of the Tala hydro project (installed capacity of 1,020 MW) in 2006 significantly increased the current energy generation (2,560 MW) by an annual average of 4,865 GWh.

Bangladesh

Bangladesh is a modest contributor to global GHG emissions, accounting for an estimated 0.4 per cent of global emissions in 2018. According to the World Bank macroeconomic projections, the GHG emissions would reach 276 $MtCO_2e$ by 2024. The growth of GHG over the past three decades was led by the energy sector, consistent with the expansion of the industrial sector and increased electricity access. GHG emissions from energy and fuel combustion activities surpassed those from agriculture in 2017 (World Bank Group, 2022). The power sector is dominated by fossil fuel-based generation. Nearly 70 per cent of primary energy consumption in 2021 was derived from natural gas, and only 1.0 per cent was derived from renewables.

Power sector emissions are forecast to grow from 20.98 $MtCO_2e$ in 2012 to 95.14 $MtCO_2e$ by 2030. In 2020, 70 per cent of electricity generation was from gas-fired plants, 23 per cent from highly polluting and expensive heavy-oil fuel plants, and 6 per cent from coal. Although the government cancelled 8.4 GW in planned coal-fired generation in June 2021, seven large coal-fired power plants currently are committed and under construction and are expected to account for up to one-third of the country's energy mix by 2025. Bangladesh maintains substantial subsidies on fossil fuel use, which create disincentives for decarbonisation. These subsidies may be explicit, when retail prices are below the supply cost of fuel's supply cost, or implicit, when the external costs of fuel use, such as impacts on climate change, are not captured in the selling price. Explicit subsidies vary based on the difference between fixed retail and wholesale prices and import prices. Bangladesh also maintains sizeable implicit subsidies on coal, diesel, and other oil consumption (Amin et al., 2022). In total, natural gas subsidies amount to an estimated 2.0 per cent of gross domestic product (GDP), diesel subsidies to 0.5 per cent of GDP, and electricity subsidies to 0.5 per cent of GDP (IMF, 2022).

Subsidised diesel prices perpetuate inefficient diesel-based irrigation systems and motorised transport. These subsidies are regressive and inefficient and could be repurposed and directed to the poor through targeted social protection programmes or incentivised transfers (Granado et al., 2010). An analysis of the removal of energy subsidies suggests that more efficient resource allocation contributes to GDP growth, with additional growth benefits if a cash transfer programme is introduced to support poor households. Subsidy elimination would increase government revenues and contribute to income distribution while helping to reduce the harmful externalities associated with the use of fossil fuels, such as mortality and morbidity associated with air pollution and CO_2 and other GHG emissions (World Bank Group, 2022).

CH_4 and CO_2 emissions in the upstream oil and gas sector (production, gathering, processing, refining, transportation, and distribution operations) contribute substantially to Bangladesh's GHG emissions. Most of the country's CO_2 emissions stem from oil and gas production and use, which generated close to 84 per cent of the country's total emissions (76.6 $MtCO_2e$) in 2020. CH_4 emissions for oil and gas operations were estimated at 408 kilotons in 2020, roughly equivalent to 11.5 $MtCO_2e$, accounting for approximately 70 per cent of total energy sector CH_4 emissions.

Decarbonisation is becoming a top priority for the country amid rising energy and material costs, resource insecurity and supply unreliability, changing preferences of global buyers, new carbon tax regimes, and national and corporate 'Net-Zero' commitments. A rapid decline in the cost of low carbon technologies (e.g. solar PV, wind, battery storage) has added to this momentum (World Bank Group, 2022). The energy sector will account for 96.1 per cent of the planned unconditional and conditional reductions by 2030 (Government of Bangladesh, 2021). The Bangladesh Sustainable and Renewable Energy Development Authority (SREDA) has developed a Building Energy and Environment Rating System for green buildings to incentivise the construction sector and material suppliers to become greener by applying more sustainable building practices. The development of renewables has been limited by the relatively high costs and the limited availability of physical infrastructure. Some progress in developing RE capacity is underway. Approximately 770 megawatts MW of RE capacity is installed, reducing GHG emissions by 3 $MtCO_2e$, and RE projects of between 1,500 and 2,000 MW are currently in development, concentrated in solar PV.

The World Bank's Scaling Up Renewable Energy Program estimates a total RE technical potential at 3.7 GW. The technical potential for rooftop PV in Dhaka alone, however, is around 7 GW, and the draft SREDA National Solar Energy Road Map 2021–2044 estimates the total PV potential at 40 GW, comprising 12 GW rooftop and 28 GW utility-scale PV. This potential could increase to 53 GW from utility-scale solar PV. Access to emerging RE technologies can add to RE use. For example, the Bhola 2 220 megawatt combined cycle power plant can operate on a dual-fuel basis of gas and high-speed diesel, although it is expected to operate primarily on gas. The plant can use hydrogen blended fuel through a gas turbine that allows it to operate on a blended fuel with up to 60 per cent of hydrogen concentration. This could result in lower CO_2 emissions but will depend upon the availability of blended fuel. With a standardised tariff of approximately USD 0.04 per kilowatt/hour, the plant is expected to function as a baseload source of power generation and provide stability to the power grid, thus supporting plans to curtail the expansion of new coal-based power generation for future baseload power needs.

India

India is one of the most dynamic and vibrant markets in the world for renewable energy. The country possesses a wealth of renewable resources, particularly for solar and bioenergy development. Greater integration of renewables would improve energy access for poor communities and boost overall energy security.

In economic terms, the increased use of renewables in 2030 would save India around 12 times more than it costs, when reduced environmental and health damage are taken into account. Savings from reduced air pollution alone would total between USD 45 billion and USD 160 billion per year. As per an analysis, along with ensuring cleaner air and water and helping to curb energy-related carbon dioxide emissions, the transition to renewable energy would create more jobs (IRENA, 2017).

India can take the lead in driving the energy transformation, both regionally and globally, with one of the largest and most ambitious renewable energy programmes anywhere in the world. It has set a target of 175 GW of installed renewable energy capacity by 2022, including 100 GW of solar, 60 GW of wind, 10 GW of biomass, and 5 GW of small hydropower. By March 2016, India's installed power generation capacity had reached 302 GW: 69 per cent of it is thermal. Most of the remainder is large hydropower (42.6 GW) and other renewables (37.4 GW). Nuclear power accounts for the remaining 2 per cent (5.8 GW). The share of renewables fluctuated between 13 per cent and 19 per cent between 2000 and 2015, meeting 17 per cent of electricity supply in 2015. According to Desert Power India, the national target is to add 455 GW of renewable energy capacity by 2050. About two-thirds of this would be installed in desert regions in the northern and western parts of the country. The plan is to use 5-15 per cent of the wasteland available in these regions to realise their large potential for solar and wind. Using 95 per cent of the available potential on 10 per cent of the area would be equivalent to 271 GW of total solar photovoltaic (PV) capacity and 29 GW of total wind.

According to the US Energy Information Administration estimates, India has more than 250 trillion cubic feet of shale gas resources in four basins, equivalent to more than 1000 years of natural gas consumption based on today's level of demand. National oil companies are allowed to explore and exploit such unconventional hydrocarbon resources (Krishnamoorthy, n.d.). India also has an installed nuclear capacity of 5 GW, with a plan to reach 60 GW by 2032.

The policy push for the RE in India has been very encouraging. The government is pushing for investments in renewable power generation technologies, amounting to USD 100 billion over the period to 2019. There is also strong financial support for renewables in the country. In 2015, clean energy investment increased to USD 10.9 billion, in line with expectations. This represented an increase from the previous two years but was still below the 2011 record of USD 13.1 billion. The amount of support received from such institutions as the US Export Bank, KfW, the Asia Development Bank (ADB), and the European Investment Bank (EIB) has reached USD 1 billion in recent years. India is also to receive funds from the World Bank to support one of its first ultra-mega solar projects, with a total installed capacity of 750 MW, in Madhya Pradesh (World Bank, 2017). The government is now permitting full foreign direct investment and is encouraging the transfer of foreign technologies, including renewables. So far, cooperation frameworks have been established with 44 countries (Ministry of New and Renewable Energy, 2022b).

Scaling up the renewable energy sector hinges on the combination of funding mechanisms, legislative frameworks, institutional arrangements, and other efforts, which work together to support implementing strategies, policies, and programmes.

Some of the negative externalities that need attention are:

Solar power system:

- Requires sizeable amount of land
- Poses environmental hazards if the production process is not handled appropriately

Hydro:

- Native population displacement
- Soil erosion

- Reduced agricultural land
- Ecosystem disturbance

Wind:

- Alteration in migrating birds' flight path
- Electromagnetic interference for radio signals
- Consequential noise from rotating blades
- Eyesore to the landscape

Biomass/Biogas:

- Fuel source uncertain and requires land for waste production
- Facility requires sizeable amount of land and water

Nepal

Nepal is a landlocked country with India and China as its southern and northern neighbours, respectively. It is one of the richest countries in the world in inland water resources with as many as 6000 rivers, rivulets, and tributaries. Nepal's perennial rivers and topography are ideal for developing hydroelectric projects. The country's hydropower potential is estimated to be upwards of 50,000 MW—the actual electricity generation from hydropower in Nepal is currently 800 MW from 20 major hydropower plants and a number of small and micro hydropower plants (International Finance Corporation, 2023). Nepal has negligible wind and fossil-energy resources. Solar energy is, by far, the largest and most sustainable energy resource in Nepal. The solar potential is about 100 times larger than that required to support a 100 per cent solar energy system in which all Nepalese citizens enjoy a similar per capita energy consumption to developed countries, without the use of fossil fuels and without the environmental degradation resulting from damming Nepal's Himalayan rivers (Lohani and Blakers, 2021). The country's untapped hydropower can play a significant role in future energy supply, as it is an affordable and renewable source of electricity with few environmental effects. It can significantly reduce the carbon footprints of neighbouring giants and one of the most populous countries, Bangladesh. It, therefore, has the potential to become a bedrock of energy security for South Asia.

Nepal has declared the Energy and Water Resources Decade (2018-28) to implement the Roadmap for Energy Development. Nepal has now become self-sufficient in electricity production, producing 11,064 GWh in 2022, a significant jump from 4,258 GWh in 2013 (Dhungel and Bhandari, 2022).

Also, Nepal is located at a latitude of 26–30° North, with the sun shining for more than 300 days per year. It has relatively high insolation of an average of ~17 megajoules per m^2 per day (1.7 TWh per km^2 per year) and national average sunshine hours of 6.8 per day. This makes Nepal a country with moderately high solar potential (Global Solar Atlas; Pondyal et al., 2011).

Having understood the status of energy composition, utilisation, and underutilisation of the energy resources of each country of BBIN, it is critical to study the significance of energy cooperation for Bangladesh, Bhutan, India, and Nepal. The next section describes this.

Significance of Energy Cooperation for Bangladesh, Bhutan, India, and Nepal

South Asia is experiencing rapid economic growth and population increase, leading to a rising energy demand. Ensuring energy security, with an emphasis on a steady supply of affordable and sustainable energy, is crucial for the region. With significant concerns about climate change, shifting to low carbon energy sources is essential to reduce environmental risks (Confederation of Indian Industries, 2023).

The fact is that no South Asian country is going to be able to meet its energy needs entirely from within its own domestic resources. India has significant coal deposits, Bangladesh has natural gas, and Bhutan and Nepal have substantial undeveloped hydropower potential (Nexant Study, 2004). Greater cooperation within South Asia could be one of the most effective ways to deal with regional energy deficits (Ahmad, 2000). A World Bank study describes such an approach as providing a "logical and rational public policy choice ... a win–win situation to all the participants" (Krishnaswamy, 2007). There are many areas where energy cooperation could be possible. This is especially important given the global uncertainties in trade, global recessionary trends, and the energy supply conundrum due to the Ukraine crisis. India offers to be the best bet in the entire scheme of things for Bangladesh, Bhutan, and Nepal. Energy security will be crucial, as any disruption in supply (as Bangladesh has been facing) may rob the sub-region of further growth opportunities and accentuate the liquidity crisis. The pipelines having been built or planned between India and these countries or in the pipeline makes regional trade a win-win for Indian refiners, given the rapid energy transition to electric, hydrogen, etc. However, the lack of infrastructure in the neighbouring economies is a major hurdle to reaching this goal. Electricity trade is not new to the sub-region. Hydroelectricity imported from Bhutan is a critical component of India's electricity basket.

India has been mitigating peak shortages in Nepal for many years. With Kathmandu adding to its hydroelectric capacities, Delhi recently created provisions for importing over 400 MW of electricity from Nepal.

In the second half of 2022, the Himalayan country exported electricity worth $83 million (INR 683 crore) to India as against its annual power import of $116 million (INR 954 crore). Energy became the third largest export revenue earner for Nepal.

India is now supplying a little less than 1,200 MW to Bangladesh. Imports contributed nearly 10 per cent of the power availability in Bangladesh in 2020. The importance of the deal became clear in 2022 when the foreign exchange crisis forced Dhaka to regulate generation from costly gas and liquid fuel, together accounting for 85 per cent of the supply in 2020.

The share of imports will rise dramatically in 2023, as Adani Power will initiate dedicated supply from a 1600 MW plant in Jharkhand. The first unit and transmission facilities on the Indian side are ready.

Essentially, it becomes evident that the scope of the trade can increase immensely if the four nations create a common or synchronous electricity grid. India and Bhutan are already running one of the oldest such cross-country grids in the world.

It is time for Bangladesh and Nepal to join the system, making it a parallel to Continental Europe Synchronous Area (CESA). A synchronous grid would ensure two-way trade and is run under a common code. It requires the participating nations to maintain the same technical and commercial standards in grid operations.

Due to a mismatch in technical standards and regulatory framework, India does electricity trade with Nepal and Bangladesh through asynchronous (limited one-way operations) mode. The sustained capacity addition by all BBIN countries, coupled with a rise in the share of renewable generation in India, is opening new opportunities for electricity trade in the region.

A common grid will help tap such opportunities, ensure energy security at optimal use of resources, and reduce carbon footprint. For example, Northeast India should be electricity-surplus with the commissioning of the first two units of the 2000 MW Lower Subansiri Hydroelectric project by June 2023. The surplus will keep rising with time as more projects are lined up in the region.

Hydroelectricity generation suffers a high degree of seasonality and peak/off-peak difference. To solve the problem, India is adding pump-storage facilities. A synchronous grid could have saved that cost by exporting the surplus to Pakistan or Nepal.

The region has immense potential to benefit from the seasonal differences in supply and demand. Bhutan and Nepal experience excess water in the summer and shortages in the winter, leading to more electricity production than needed in the summer and less in the winter. Due to India's hot summers and Bhutan's and Nepal's cold winters, the electricity demand patterns align well between these countries and several Indian regions. Year-round cross-border electricity trade can also boost the utilisation of power plants, particularly in the less industrialised areas of Bhutan and Nepal, during off-peak hours (Vaidya et al., 2018).

Asynchronous trade limits this prospect, as every export or import operation needs the creation of new interconnections, which are costly, time-taking, and lack flexibility (Bose, 2023). Sub-regional energy cooperation would help optimise resources and improve intraregional trade by reducing costs and import dependence. It would improve efficiency in the power sector and strengthen energy security during external shocks or volatile petroleum prices. It would enhance regional power exchange structures and also increase access and development of renewable energy resources, helping protect an increasingly fragile environment (SASEC, 2013).

This book is organised as follows: Chapter 1 provides a detailed understanding of the resurgence of sub-regionalism in the form of BBIN, juxtaposing it with the shortcomings of SAARC. It provides a vivid picture of the status of energy composition, utilisation, and underutilisation of the energy resources of each country of BBIN. It delineates the characteristic features of BBIN and situates the significance and unlocking the cooperation potential in the sub-region, especially with respect to renewable energy in the Sustainable Development Goal era. Supported by exhaustive literature on theories of sub-regionalism in international relations, Chapter 2 provides an in-depth understanding of what the concept entails. References have been made to similar efforts undertaken around the world to foster sub-regional groupings. Lessons would be drawn from such experiments and their efficiencies would be assessed by their tenacity in the face of the various challenges. Chapter 3 discusses the different areas of energy cooperation, namely, power; oil and gas; and new and renewable energy sources, for each of the BBIN countries. The various high-level meetings that have been held and the agreements signed and undertaken under the BBIN framework have been analysed to validate the buoyancy of the political will to forge a potent sub-regional grouping. Chapter 4 makes unbiased assessments of the energy cooperation in BBIN based on extensive review of literature and data from official and secondary sources. This would provide a logical conduit for Chapter 5, which contains the policy recommendations as the way forward, followed by conclusions to sum up the major findings of the book and apprise any major latest event in the context of BBIN energy cooperation. This study employs qualitative research methodology in understanding the BBIN as a sub-regional framework for energy cooperation. Secondary data were evaluated rigorously, and arguments were developed based on the content analysis of each source collected. To explain the status, prospects, and challenges of energy cooperation in the sub-region, interviews were conducted in India, Nepal, Bhutan, and Bangladesh. The study placed emphasis on the subjective experiences of individuals and the use of broad, open-ended questions to understand the views as well as opinions of the experts. Informed consent was obtained from interview respondents prior to undertaking the research through email as well as before the beginning of the face-to-face interviews. The interviews were recorded manually and a simple process of coding was used to identify particular themes that were highlighted by the respondents.

Face-to-face discussions were held with 10 Nepali hydropower developers, planners, and investment specialists from the private sector and government functionaries from the Nepal Electricity Authority (NEA) in Kathmandu, Nepal, in June 2022 and 8 Bangladeshi experts from think tanks, government training institutes, and the Bangladesh Energy Regulatory Commission. They included founders and managing directors, chief operating officers, and chief financial officers of Nepali hydropower development companies. All respondents comprised senior management and had, on average, more than 20 years of professional experience in the hydropower sector. Their educational background varied from economics, finance, and business management to civil engineering and hydraulics; the majority had a master's degree (nine respondents), seven respondents had a PhD, and the rest had a bachelor's degree. Three respondents had vast experience in the domestic hydropower sector of Nepal and Bangladesh. The sampling of respondents was purposive, given the niche character of the research topic. Most of the respondents were approached via snowballing. The respondents spoke in a personal capacity and as anonymous responses not wanting to be quoted, which not only reflected both their experience in the hydropower business and their broader concern for the economic development of Nepal and Bangladesh but more importantly, their concern to safely function in their countries. The statements and opinions are incorporated in the various chapters outlined above.

Notes

1. SAARC Charter, https://www.saarc-sec.org/index.php/resources/agreements-conventions/46-saarc-charter-provisional-rules-of-procedure/file
2. MWp is a measure of the maximum potential output of power.

2

Theorising Sub-regionalism in the Study of International Relations

At the global level, when the gamut of interrelationships between states is viewed as an international system, there are groups at the regional level that form international sub-systems. These sub-systems or 'regions' are not only important in balancing the power equations at the global level but also in shaping the socio-economic and political destinies of the constituent nations. Although geographical proximity and contiguity in themselves indicate little about either the definitions of regions or the dynamics of regionalism, they are helpful in distinguishing regionalism from other forms of 'less than global' organisation. Without some geographical limits, the term 'regionalism' becomes diffuse and unmanageable (Hurrell, 1995; Mansfield and Milner, 1997).

Over the last two decades, there has been a veritable explosion of research and policy discussion on regional integration and regionalism all over the world. Some of the most influential thinkers in the field emphasise that regions and regionalism are now central to global politics. For instance, Katzenstein (2005) rejected the "purportedly stubborn persistence of the nation-state or the inevitable march of globalisation", arguing that we are approaching a "world of regions". Acharya (2007) examined the "emerging regional architecture of world politics". Buzan and Weaver (2003) highlighted the global order of strong regions. According to Fawn (2009), regions are present everywhere across the globe and are increasingly fundamental to the functioning of all aspects of world affairs from trade to conflict management and can even be said to now constitute world order.

Regionalism

Regionalism is an emergent art of international government. It represents a different mode of exercising authority across international space and of integrating poorer populations (Larner and Walters, 2002). Regionalism has most often been analysed in terms of social cohesiveness (ethnicity, race, language, religion, culture, history, consciousness of a common heritage), economic cohesiveness (trade patterns, economic complementarity), political cohesiveness (regime type, ideology), and organisational cohesiveness (existence of formal regional institutions) (Russet, 1969). In all this, regional interdependence gained popularity (Nye, 1968). Regionalism has positive implications on the constituent nation states when it is perceived to be morally correct as a description rather than being perceived as a prescription, i.e., how the relations between them 'ought' to be organised. In other words, it implies a strong sense that the states of a given region are all in the same regional boat, ecologically, strategically, and economically, and that they are not pulling together, but, either explicitly stated or implied, should put aside national egoisms and devise new forms of cooperation (Hurrell, 1995).

Regionalisation refers to the growth of societal integration within a region and to the often undirected processes of social and economic interaction. The term lays particular weight on autonomous economic processes, which lead to higher levels of economic integration and interdependence within a given region, i.e., a geographical area, rather than between that area and the rest of the world (Hormats, 1995).

Regionalisation consists of processes that generate an order for which rules of governance or even creation of formal institutions—either formal or informal, involving patterns of regular meetings with some rules attached, together with mechanisms for preparation and follow-up—are established by relevant authoritative actors to achieve certain mutually agreed ends (Lawson, 2009). A great deal of regionalist activity involves the negotiation and construction of interstate or intergovernmental agreements or regimes.

Such cooperative arrangements can serve a wide variety of purposes. On the one hand, they can serve as a means of responding to external challenges and of coordinating regional positions in international institutions or negotiating forums. On the other hand, they can be developed to secure welfare gains, to promote common values, or to solve common problems, especially problems arising from increased levels of regional interdependence (Warleigh-Lack, 2006). It may lead to the development of trans-border growth triangles, industrial corridors, or the increasingly dense networks linking major industrial centres (Hurrell, 1995).

The new regionalism approach (NRA) seeks to describe this multidimensional process of regionalisation in terms of levels of "region-ness", the process whereby a geographical area is transformed from a passive object to an active subject, capable of articulating transnational interests (Hettne and Söderbaum, 2000; Söderbaum, 2013).

Regional integration involves specific policy decisions by governments, designed to reduce or remove trade barriers to mutual exchange of goods, services, capital, and people and the formation of a customs union in goods. The European Union (EU) is generally taken as an example par excellence of formal regionalisation, while organisations like the Association of Southeast Asian Nations (ASEAN) have historically been far more informal with respect to rules of governance. The strong rule-based and heavily institutionalised approach of the EU is often taken to be more distinctively 'Western' in political style, while with ASEAN, the notion that it proceeds only on the basis of a consensus among members is said to reflect the cultural values of the region (Haacke, 2003; Acharya, 2004). It is understood to be a norm of diplomacy, incorporating, among other things, 'consensus building through non-conflictual discussion' (Haas, 1989). The EU reveals a complex mixture of traditional intergovernmentalism and emerging supranationalism arising out of regional cohesion (Hurrell, 1995).

According to neo-realists, European integration, which was, in reality, sub-regional integration, was embedded within a transatlantic security framework and 'outside-in' pressures continued to influence the path of its integration. It was seen as a means of countering the 'exorbitant privilege' of the United States. The same neo-realist logic can also be applied to the policies of smaller states outside Europe. According to this view, many regionalist groupings are basically the natural response of weak states trapped in the world of the strong (Hurrell, 1995).

Constructivist theories focus on regional awareness and regional identity, on the shared sense of belonging to a particular regional community, and on what has been called 'cognitive regionalism'. They stress the extent to which regional cohesion depends on a sustained and durable sense of community based on mutual responsiveness, trust, and high levels of what might be called 'cognitive interdependence'. Instead of focusing solely on material incentives, constructivists emphasise the importance of shared knowledge, learning, ideational forces, and normative and institutional structures (Wendt, 1995).

Regionalism is more appropriately used to denote an ideological package of values, beliefs, motives, and interests, underpinning invocations of a region and the processes, activities, and institutions which constitute 'the region' as a tangible entity. It is "naturalised" through geographical proximity and the mobilisation of shared identities. The developmentalism approach to regionalism highlights that the vocabulary of regionalism also includes that of market economics, including of growth, dynamism, and prosperity, and only sometimes, of a regional sense of community and identity (Larner and Walters, 2002).

Both regionalisation (as a process) and regionalism (as a set of discourses) together produce 'the region' and constitute regional identities. It must be noted that identities generally exhibit three basic characteristics. First, identity formation is relational; the process requires a contrasting image against which self-identity can be constructed—the 'self/other' dimension common to virtually every form of identity politics. Second, identities are situational; they may be activated according to the demands of a particular context. Third, identities are often instrumental; they can be deployed strategically in the pursuit of goals or as defensive mechanisms in the face of unwelcome external pressures (Lawson, 2006).

Regional cooperation refers to countries coming together in joint efforts to address common problems or to make use of opportunities. Regional cooperation produces results and incurs costs that are typically unevenly spread across the group of countries; thus, considerable negotiation is required in any regional effort to ensure that all perceive that the effort merits the expense. Examples of regional cooperation initiatives include: (i) cross-border infrastructure, such as transborder bridges or roads and transmission lines; (ii) free trade agreements that jointly set the policy environment governing trade in goods or services between countries; (iii) cooperation to reduce the spread or impact of pandemics, such as avian influenza; and (iv) collective efforts to contain transboundary pollution.

As suggested by the above examples, regional cooperation can come in many forms, depending on the particular group of countries and the purpose for their collective action. According to the ADB's Regional and Subregional Economic Cooperation Programs, such collective action may be categorised into four pillars (ADB, 2012), namely:

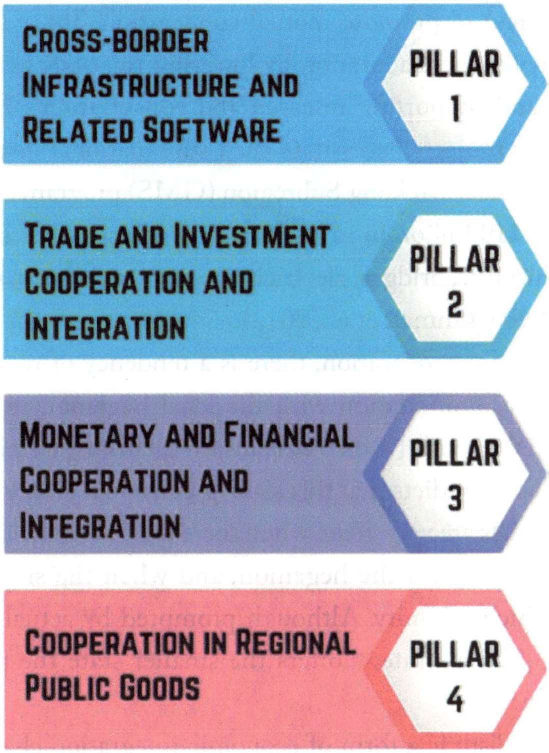

Three of the main pillars focus on activities within the energy sector. Pillar 1, for example, addresses the infrastructure for cross-border electricity transmission systems and pipelines. Pillar 2 is concerned with fostering regional trade in resources like electricity, petroleum, and natural gas. Pillar 4 involves collaborative efforts in building capacity and conducting research on topics, such as solar technology, mitigating climate change impacts, and developing technical standards that facilitate the interconnection of gas pipelines and transmission lines. Regional cooperation serves as a complementary approach to national programmes and policies in achieving national objectives. This is where regional institutions come into play. The term "regional" implies a supranational initiative, which can be exemplified by organisations, such as the United

Nations, designed to promote mutual cooperation. These supranational bodies can facilitate collaboration by lowering the costs associated with negotiations and supporting research and consultations. However, not all cross-border projects necessitate such supranational institutions. For instance, the Greater Mekong Subregion (GMS) program has effectively managed over $10 billion in investments for cross-border infrastructure projects like airports, bridges, electricity transmission lines, railways, and roads since 1990 (Rahman et al., 2012).

In sub-regional cooperation, there is a tendency of weaker states to seek regional accommodation with the local hegemon in the hope of receiving special rewards ('bandwagoning' in the realist terminology). The neo-realist theory predicts that this kind of behaviour is most likely when power differentials are very great, when there are few external alternatives to accommodation with the hegemon, and when the small state is in close geographic proximity. Although prompted by actual or potential vulnerability, such a strategy offers the smaller state the possibility of material benefit.

Sub-regionalism is a form of economic integration characterised by a sense of unanimity, less formal arrangements, geographical proximity, and a controlled regional development strategy, propelled by a willingness and urgency to promote development with a focus on smaller growth-oriented zones within a broader region to enhance their competitiveness and promote their exports in the global market (Murthy, 2008). Sub-regionalism is a case of the market in juxtaposition to institutional integration, where legal agreements encourage preferential trade among member countries. Member countries rely on non-official institutions to provide public and semi-public goods, lowering transaction costs related to the international movement of goods and services and other production costs. Member nations give specific projects or initiatives in crucial economic sectors utmost importance as they will support and complement their national plans and strategies and effectively use local synergies and affinities. Ultimately, such groupings are deemed to boost trade relations by contributing tangible progress in the respective nations (Nepali, 2023).

Subregional cooperation came into being in the 1990s. The reasons for its creation varied according to the regions in which it developed. In East and Southeast Asia, economic considerations were the primary factors that gave rise to subregional cooperation. In Europe, however, its development can be majorly attributed to political and security compulsions. Subregional patterns enlarge the concept of proximity to encompass factors other than geographic distance. Indeed, historical legacies and economic forces can provide the propellants for the migration of industries, employment creation, and spill-over to other areas (Mittleman, 1996). For instance, sub-regional economic zones transcend political boundaries but need not involve entire national economies. Rather, they intersect only the border areas of the national economies (Yue and Yuan, 1993).

Contemporary sub-regionalism is multifaceted and diverse and forms a response to both the process of increasing economic globalisation and the need to deal with economic underdevelopment. Within sub-regionalism, there is a strong emphasis on cooperation as an alternative to a formal alliance system; as such, sub-regionalism is based on less formal structures than old regionalism (Hook and Kearns (eds.), 1999). Manoli (2012) defined sub-regionalism as a process of regularised but significant political and economic interaction between a group of neighbouring states but with the interaction taking place at different levels, including national governments and local authorities, as well as private businesses and civil society actors, with a focus on policy coordination. Another definition of sub-regionalism describes it as a process for responding to transnational policy challenges and addressing specific demands, related to economic, environmental, borders and customs, energy or infrastructure issues, or for supporting tourism and culture at the local level (Ngampramuan and Ploberger, 2020). Likewise, it has also been understood that sub-regionalism focuses on economic development, transnational planning for infrastructure and transport, environmental problems and natural resource management, and facilitating human contacts, especially in the field of tourism and culture (Bremner and Bailes, 1998).

The idea of region or sub-region combines both virtual as well as material elements and is amenable rather than fixed (Paasi, 2009). A sub-region is defined, at least, partly in terms of its enormous cultural and linguistic diversity where one's primary identity is based on the commonality, which denotes a set of relationships incorporating mutual obligations based on a shared identity, usually incorporating kinship ties, language, a common geographical origin, and/or common membership of a religious group. Thus, commonality unites people in mutually supportive social networks, although it also provides the basis for hostility to other groups (Nanau, 2011, p. 32).

Since the early 1990s, East Asian countries, led by the People's Republic of China (PRC) and Singapore, increasingly focused their energy on the emergence of 'growth triangles' (Tang and Thant, 1994). Growth triangles extend across the national borders of geographically proximate countries. Sub-regional cooperation in trade does not involve the participation of the entire member country, unlike regional trading agreements. Thus, for example, in the BBIN framework, states, such as Uttar Pradesh and Bihar, and the north-eastern region ought to be the participating provinces that represent India in the grouping.

The purpose behind growth triangles entails member countries to jointly cooperate on exploiting factor endowments present across their geographies (Tang and Thant, 1994). Subregional trade agreements, like other multilateral trade agreements, are promoted with the explicit purpose of enhancing trade, investments, and development. Apart from geographical proximities, subregional groupings also help leverage cultural proximities that may enable faster and efficient developmental projects.

The end of the Cold War and the breakout of the Yugoslav and Balkan Wars left behind a trail of institutional handicaps and transnational crimes, such as trafficking of weapons and drugs. These cumulative factors led the post-Soviet countries to enter into subregional cooperation to better tackle them. According to Cottey (2009), there were potentially four reasons that led to the emergence of subregional cooperation in Europe. These were: political confidence-building measures, creation of subregional frameworks as a path towards membership of the European Union, need to better tackle transnational issues of environment and economy, and need to help the war-ravaged and post-Soviet countries to transition to market economies.

The Baltic Cooperation of Estonia, Latvia, and Lithuania was one such sub-regional cooperation established in 1994. The three countries used their sub- regional framework to project a cooperative image of themselves to gain membership into larger multilateral organisations, such as the European Union (EU) and the North Atlantic Treaty Organization (NATO).

The major challenge in fostering a sub-regional collaboration is that of national interests vis-à-vis collective interests, which are unlikely to simply disappear. Taken together, such tensions mean that all will not be smooth sailing in the regional and sub-regional politics of South Asia, BBIN, or any other sub-regional framework in the foreseeable future. Overall, the challenges to sub-regional collaboration can be described through the mainstream theories of international relations, namely, liberalism, realism, and constructivism. The following section describes how the former two are limited in understanding the obstacles to energy cooperation in BBIN, and therefore, highlights that a constructivist approach can best explain the constraints.

Theories on Challenges to Energy Cooperation in BBIN

The two main schools of thought in international relations theories, liberalism and realism, provide diverse perceptions of the possibility of cooperation, influenced by their varied interpretation of world affairs. While realism is based on the notion that the absence of a global authority (anarchy) renders cooperation extremely difficult and limited, liberals argue that due to the interest of states in mutually beneficial outcomes, cooperation is highly possible despite the anarchy of the global system (Viotti and Kauppi, 2012). The regime theory, which conceptualises the modalities of international organisations, has both liberal and realist interpretations, with liberals stressing the role of international organisations in creating an environment conducive to cooperation while realists insist that regimes are merely an extension of a state's national interests (Dunne et al., 2013).

These mainstream theories of international relations are limited in accounting for the political obstacles to energy cooperation in South Asia. Approaching challenges to cooperation from the realist perspective implies that constraints imposed by anarchy and the security dilemma are inevitable and exist independently of the social, cultural, and historical constituents of the region. On the other hand, the explanations offered by liberalism regarding the challenges to cooperation, such as lack of reciprocity, misinformation, and miscommunication, paints a rather simplistic view of geopolitics. The underlying assumption in both approaches that states, as rational actors, will undertake cost-benefit analyses on entering into cooperation with other states paints a limited and simplistic vision of the origins of state interests.

Enhancing regional cooperation and integration in resource sharing, production, and trade can create a network of interdependence among countries, maximising resource use. Liberals, functionalists, and neo-functionalists believe that cooperation in one sector can lead to cooperation in other areas. The functionalist approach suggests focusing on areas of common interest first and leaving contentious issues aside. This interconnectedness is expected to lead to more harmonious relations between states, aligning with the liberal idea that trade promotes peace (Gartzke and Li, 2003; Mansfield and Pollins, 2001). However, while balanced trade relations can foster peace, imbalanced trade, where one party depends heavily on another, can negatively impact peace prospects (Barbieri, 1996). In the BBIN sub-region, energy trade and investment represent areas of mutual dependence and common interest, potentially enhancing overall cooperation and interaction in other sectors.

In a critique of the universal applicability of Western-centric schools of thought, Sondhi (2006) has stated that the sovereign state that lies at the heart of contemporary international relations theories is at odds with the weak nature of governance in South Asian countries and the fact that internal security concerns in these countries far outweigh issues, such as the international balance of power. The author makes a convincing case for a constructivist approach in coming to terms with the identities and interests of South Asian countries.

Within the constructivist theorem, the world is perceived to be constituted through social interaction; agents and structures are perceived as mutually constituted; and the centrality of identity and norms in world politics is stressed (Checkel, 1998; McDonald, 2013).

The unique socio-cultural aspects of the subcontinent and its millennium-old geographic continuity that was violently disrupted in 1947 has left an endemic mark in South Asia, where the influence of history, religion, society, ethnicity, class, caste, and other endogenic factors greatly influences the outcomes of negotiations. Constructivism is arguably a more suitable approach in coming to terms with the challenges to South Asian energy cooperation, especially as it points to the importance of ideational factors, including norms and identity, which can be constitutive of the national interest and global politics more broadly (McDonald, 2013, p. 64).

Constructivists perceive the world to be constituted through inter-subjective interaction and believe agents and structures as mutually constituted (McDonald, 2013). Wendt (1992) has argued that structural issues, such as anarchy, in the global system are not static and are influenced by the actions of agents. This flexible interpretation of structures and an emphasis on the way structures and agents influence each other allows for perceiving challenges to cooperation as an interlinked web, where each component influences the other. This is a closer analogy of the subject matter of energy cooperation than the static perception of structural issues in orthodox accounts of foreign policy.

Overall, while the various theories of international relations have tried to explain the impediments to cooperation, the complex energy projects being planned in the unique geopolitical region of South Asia has resulted in challenges that are contextually diverse and vital in theory development. As such, the political challenges associated with the various energy projects in South Asia require detailed exposition.

Depending upon the geography, a sub-regional framework focuses on issues of mutual concern, such as energy cooperation, infrastructure development, fisheries management, trade and investment, sustainable development, aviation and shipping facilities, a regional coastguard project, educational facilities, energy supply, climate change and rising sea levels, and cooperation with the wider regional bodies, for instance, in the case of BBIN, SAARC and BIMSTEC (Lawson, 2016).

Partnerships of the sustainable energy paradigm involve multiple organisations with complementary competences (Newell et al., 2009; Sovacool, 2012). For instance, international partnerships between governments, multilateral agencies, and development banks set up renewable energy technologies (RET) programme frameworks and funding streams. Regional and national partnerships translate global initiatives into national and local programmes and initiate additional national programmes. Partnerships of this kind may involve different types of donor organisations, governmental agencies, banks and micro-finance institutions, utilities, universities, firms, and NGOs. Finally, there are project partnerships that implement projects derived from RET programmes and smaller initiatives. Project partnerships further extend the range of partners to local businesses, community-based organisations, and groups of end-users.

Renewable energy partnerships at all levels vary in their focus and intensity as the partnership label is used for continuous and close collaborations as well as for roundtables, repeat contracting and consulting (Forsyth, 2010; van Huijstee et al., 2007). In this way, the meaning of the term 'partnership' appears to be blurred, covering close alliances as well as arm's length market relationships (Vincent and Byrne, 2006). This is in stark contrast to the way the term is used across much of the academic literature, where 'partnerships' in development cooperation generally imply "a joint commitment to long-term interaction, shared responsibility for achievement, reciprocal obligation, equality, mutuality and balance of power" (Fowler, 2000). Studies of partnerships in development cooperation have revealed a frequent gap between the rhetoric and reality of cross-sector partnerships, with many partnerships being defined by the bureaucratic demands of donor organisations rather than partnership principles (Ashman, 2001; Elbers et al., 2014; Ellersiek, 2011; Fowler, 2000; Lister, 2000; Vincent and Byrne, 2006).

A case in point here is that of Bangladesh. Electricity demand in Bangladesh is much higher than the electricity generation capacity of the country. The generation of electricity in Bangladesh mainly depends on natural gas that is a non-renewable resource. In 2017, the total electricity generation capacity was 13,621 MW, of which natural gas contributed 62.62 per cent. This is an unsustainable and alarming trend for Bangladesh, because after 15–20 years, natural gas reserves in the country will run out. The electricity demand of Bangladesh in 2035 will be around 87,991 MW. In this situation, it is urgent to find ways to fulfil the future electricity demand of Bangladesh and explore to what extent hydropower development could help meet the energy demand in Bangladesh. Nepal, Bhutan, and India have huge hydropower potential. After meeting domestic electricity demand, these hydropower-rich countries could export excess electricity to neighbouring countries like Bangladesh and India (Rahaman and Hossain, 2020). However, the caveat remains. While hydropower is a clean and renewable source of energy, there are environmental challenges to its long-term sustainability. Extreme events, such as glacial lake outburst floods, floods, landslides, and climate-induced variation in the hydrological regime, pose threats to hydropower projects (Pokharel, 2001) by shortening their useful lifetime (Ray et al., 2018) and reducing production capacity (Bhatt, 2017). For the sustainability of hydropower in the region, it is important to minimise environmental threats and also consider the possibility of taking advantage of some of the related changes (Vaidya et al., 2021). According to the International Hydropower Association (IHA), risk can be mitigated through both structural (e.g. sediment settling basin, erosion protection works) and non-structural measures (e.g. legal instruments, operating rules) (IHA, 2019). Renewable energy partnerships of the 'sustainable energy paradigm' are usually defined in terms of their expected potential to overcome the four crucial gaps outlined in the previous section (Pinkse and Kolk, 2012): First, they are envisaged to reduce resource gaps by attracting investment and creating innovative cost-sharing models. Second, partnerships are expected to foster knowledge transfer and capacity building, thus diminishing capacity gaps. Third, partnerships are thought to enhance the integration of donor-initiated and private markets and to enable a more meaningful involvement of local stakeholders, thereby closing crucial implementation gaps (Forsyth, 2010). Fourth, through networking and advocacy, partnerships may also contribute to the development of institutions addressing regulatory gaps. Following this description, partnerships of the 'sustainable energy paradigm' differ from previous forms of technical assistance in that they acknowledge the pivotal role of relationships between organisations in catalysing the multiple processes of technology diffusion. Existing empirical research on renewable energy partnerships has focused on international partnerships between policy makers in global climate governance (Bäckstrand, 2008; Newell et al., 2009; Pinkse and Kolk, 2012; Szulecki et al., 2011).

Understanding Constraints in Sub-Regional Renewable Energy Partnerships

Successful diffusion of renewable energy technologies, to a large extent, depends on the creation of appropriate inter-organisational relationships. Different types of relationships perform different functions. Strong ties facilitate fine-grained knowledge transfer, extensive collaboration, and the development of problem–solving capacities, whereas weak ties enhance access to non-redundant information and prevent the insulation of more durable renewable energy partnerships from the wider sector. Based on this analysis, we can identify different types of partnerships failures. First, there are failures that result from a lack of connectivity, i.e., the absence of ties where they are needed in order to develop and better integrate an emerging RET sector—a network failure that has also been identified by Caniëls and Romijn (2008). Second, there are partnership failures that occur because organisations have established relationships that are inappropriate for the tasks they are meant to perform. For example, partnerships aiming at the sustainable diffusion of a new technology are likely to fail if they do not develop ties that are strong enough to facilitate the kind of knowledge exchange needed to fully embed the technology in a new context.

It must be noted that large-scale energy projects are bound to face enormous challenges, cost overruns, delays, and further complications, and most of it is due to the existing systems of governance. According to Flyvbjerg (2014) , these projects are 'large-scale, complex ventures that typically cost a billion dollars or more, take many years to develop and build, involve multiple public and private stakeholders, are transformational, and impact millions of people'. But if countries and respective institutions do undertake collaborations, it becomes a good learning experience for all parties involved: a. they learn to deliver on preconceived projects; b. through capacity-building measures, project implementation improves; and c. local stakeholders receive technical assistance to successfully engage with local institutions and communities, which ultimately strengthens the agencies involved (Kruckenberg, 2015). Thus, such collaborations also bring to the fore the theories of regional governance that study the process of coordination across partner countries in a region to produce mutually agreeable regulations on important issues, including the exchange of goods and services and addressing common challenges, for instance, energy cooperation, electricity trade, transmission grids, etc. (Borzel and Risse, 2016).

The next chapter (Chapter 3) delves into the implementation of such sub-regional governance in embarking upon how a sub-regional framework continues to forge ahead in the implementation of energy cooperation between Bangladesh, Bhutan, India, and Nepal.

3

Pillars of Energy Cooperation in BBIN

Cross-border energy cooperation in the BBIN sub-region offers a unique opportunity for the member states to collaborate, integrate, and harness their diverse energy mix. Further, the RE potential of each nation presents prospects of trade that would enable a mega deployment and integration of renewable energy sources to meet the growing energy needs not only by individual countries but also by the sub-region as a whole, thereby promoting sustainability. For instance, in the electricity trade, especially in joint hydropower projects, countries can benefit mutually. This collaboration can lead to increased energy trade, with production costs decreasing over the long run. Countries can tap into one other's strengths and resources, leading to a win-win situation, percolating down to the grassroots level. Though currently, bilateral power trade prevails, there is a need to establish and open power markets, which would happen only through multilateral power trading.

Within South Asia, the Bangladesh, Bhutan, India and Nepal (BBIN) sub-region is the first to demonstrate cooperation in cross-border energy trade. This is because of the persistent problems between India and Pakistan that have jeopardised the greater goal of regional security, including energy security for the populace (Dash, 2008). Hence, it is important that the interconnected states, namely, Bangladesh,

Bhutan, India, and Nepal (BBIN), work systematically to mitigate risks to stability and order in the region (Muzaffar et al., 2017). Ever since the idea of BBIN was first floated in 1996, there have been several efforts by the constituent countries as well as multilateral institutions to streamline energy cooperation in the sub-region. While the process has taken a long time towards fruition, yet, regular negotiations amongst and between these countries have always been productive and paved the way for an affirmative future.

A Joint Statement of the Third Joint Working Group (JWG) meeting on Sub-Regional Cooperation between BBIN on water resources management and power/hydropower and on connectivity and transit was issued at the Dhaka meeting in January 2016. It discussed power trade and inter-grid connectivity cooperation in future power projects and water resources management among the four countries. The JWG decided that an Experts' Group would be constituted for exchanging best practices in water resources management and on specifics of the identified projects, power trade, inter grid connectivity, flood forecasting, and other areas of possible cooperation (Embassy of India, Thimphu, 2016).

For instance, at present, India imports power from Bhutan and Nepal and exports it to Bangladesh and Nepal. In the future, the sub-region expects to develop broader arrangements for cross-border electricity trade (CBET) based on grid interconnections, by which energy produced in Nepal and Bhutan can be sold in India and Bangladesh (Dhakal et al., 2019; Haran, 2018b).

Under the initiative of the Asian Development Bank (ADB), SASEC was initiated in 2001 with four member countries, Bangladesh, India, Bhutan, and Nepal. The ADB serves as the Secretariat for SASEC. It focuses on regional cooperation in the areas of energy, transport, and trade facilitation (and tourism in the initial years). Under the SASEC programme, the ADB provided technical, advisory, and financial support to this initiative. Energy cooperation is a main focus of the SASEC programme. The rationale behind this was that the existing intraregional energy trade among the SASEC countries was limited to electricity trade between India-Bhutan and India-Nepal (in 2011, within the framework of SASEC cooperation, it was around 5,600 gigawatt-hour (GWh) and 700 GWh, respectively); and trade in petroleum products between India and Nepal, Bhutan, Bangladesh, and Sri Lanka. It underscored that the enhanced electricity trade will be based on the expansion of power transfer links between Bhutan and India, and India and Nepal. SASEC aims to promote regional prosperity and improve economic opportunities through strengthened cross-border links in trade, power, and road and rail networks.

Some efforts for fostering energy cooperation include the India-Bangladesh power trade agreement, where the latter imports up to 500 MW power from India under an ADB loan assistance of US$ 112 million, agreed upon in 2013. In 2015, the ADB further sought to increase the transmission capacity from 500 megawatts (MW) to 1,000 MW of the cross-border electricity link between India and Bangladesh, which will allow Bangladesh to better meet the sharply rising power demand and support increased power exchanges across South Asia.

The ADB's loan of $120 million to Bangladesh was aimed to double the capacity of the existing interconnection system, which links the power grid of western Bangladesh at Bheramara and the grid of eastern India at Bharampur. In this project, the Government of Bangladesh provided a financing of $63.2 million. It has been highlighted that Bangladesh can seek convergence around cross-border transmission connectivity (with fair, open, non-discriminatory, reciprocal access and congestion management); identify opportunities for sharing generation reserves and backup capacity; and clear transmission and trade tariff regimes with standardised contractual framework documents for electricity trade. In essence, expanded access to clean power sources in India, Nepal, and Bhutan will support an increased share of green and least-cost energy in the energy mix; displacement of costlier and dirtier power generation; the phasing-out of dilapidated and highly inefficient gas-based steam turbines; and reduce demand on scarce land resources (World Bank Group, 2022). It must be recalled that these two networks were first interconnected in 2013 under the SASEC programme and previous project financing by the lending institution (ADB, 2015).

This grid-to-grid connection has significantly improved power supply and cost and reduced power interruptions in Bangladesh, where shortages were rampant at the time. While smaller countries like Nepal could potentially rely on the market to provide reserve generation capacity, thereby lowering its own investment costs, fossil fuel-based generation in Bangladesh and India could be replaced with cleaner hydropower from Bhutan and Nepal. The Siliguri corridor for Nepal-Bangladesh energy trade was only recently opened by India (Rijal, 2019). In September 2019, the India-Nepal oil pipeline, funded by India, was inaugurated by Indian Prime Minister Narendra Modi and his Nepal counterpart, K.P. Sharma Oli (Sharma, 2019).

If the access to the corridor for Bangladesh, Bhutan, and Nepal is sustained, it would prove to be an extremely positive and enabling opportunity for BBIN to gain a clean energy surplus for their populations. Further, an interconnected cross-border transmission capacity to share power with each other could lead to an interconnected power market.

The region has transitioned from deep scepticism of cross-border electricity trade to around 1,500 MW of high-voltage transmission connectivity between Bangladesh and India (1,160 MW) and Nepal and India (300 MW). To unlock the potential for regional power trade, cross-border grid interconnection needs expansion and standardisation for technically feasible, reliable, safe, and economical power exchange. The market is dominated by each country's public sector, with a few private developers from India, local (largely public sector) financiers, and international financial institutions (World Bank Group, 2022).

While a government-level push from these four countries is extremely important, investment in energy projects with public and private sector participation would unleash opportunities to focus on reliable and clean energy infrastructure projects—for example, in electricity, hydropower and natural gas transmission and distribution, civil nuclear energy, etc.—and directly and indirectly serve the population of BBIN, enabling their transition to high-performing, low-emission, and energy- secure economies.

The section below discusses the energy sector of the BBIN countries.

Bangladesh

According to Enerdata (2021), natural gas is the main energy source (59 per cent), ahead of oil (18 per cent), biomass (17 per cent), and coal (4 per cent), for electricity production. By 2020, 96 per cent of the population of Bangladesh had access to electricity, and the total final energy consumption (TFEC) from the RE sources was 25 per cent, according to the International Renewable Energy Agency. Ninety-nine per cent of the electricity generation (83,964 GWh) in the country is from non-RE sources, and the rest (1 per cent, i.e., 1175 GWh) is from RE sources: hydro and marine (777 GWh); solar (389 GWh); wind (5 GWh); and bioenergy (4 GWh) (IRENA, 2022a). At present, 88 per cent of the power plants are run by natural gas.

The need for energy in Bangladesh continues to rise. According to the International Energy Agency (2020), the total energy consumption in the country in 1990 was 5.14 TWh, and this rose to 82.01 TWh in 2020. The largest consumers of energy are the industrial and the residential sectors, followed by the commercial and public services and the agricultural sector. In 2020, the industrial and residential sectors consumed 252589 TJ of energy, while the commercial and public services and the agricultural sectors consumed 23245 TJ and 5519 TJ, respectively (IEA, 2020). Though the domestic energy production has witnessed a rise, i.e., from 450.49 TJ in 1990 to 1260.22 TJ in 2020, yet, the rising energy consumption, as highlighted above, makes Bangladesh highly dependent upon energy imports. The net energy imports have also risen. In 1990, the net energy imports were 90400 TJ, which increased to 644300 TJ in 2020.

This brings to the fore the importance and urgency of harnessing energy sources from the neighbourhood, and the sub-regional framework offers a glimmer of hope. The huge potential of hydropower and thermal sources in the neighbouring countries, such as India, Nepal and Bhutan, can be utilised by Bangladesh to meet its electricity requirement. Hence, in such a scenario, it is evident that the neighbouring countries of Bangladesh can play a vital role to meet the ever growing energy demand of Bangladesh. In fact, the construction of electrical interconnections among the neighbouring countries has become an urgent necessity for significant benefits to the sub-region through closer cooperation on regional power transfer, enhanced system reliability, improved security and diversity of supply, and increased economic efficiency in systems operations, leading to reduced environmental impacts and lower costs to consumers.

Bhutan

Bhutan's energy sector relies almost exclusively on hydropower. It has a feasible hydro-potential of 23,760 megawatts (MW) from 76 hydro schemes (greater than 10 MW capacity). The present total installed capacity of the existing hydropower plants in Bhutan is about 2326 MW (9.79 per cent) (Central Electricity Authority, 2021).

The entire population of Bhutan has access to electricity, which is met by hydropower. The TFEC from RE sources in 2019 was 82 per cent. Total energy supply in 2019 was 80505 TJ, which increased from 66291 TJ in 2014. The share of RE declined to 84 per cent in 2019 from 86 per cent in 2014. This implies that the share of non-renewables increased. The non-renewables comprise oil, gas, coal, and others. The industrial and residential sectors are the major consumers of RE. In

2014, industries consumed 7996 TJ of RE, which increased to 13212 TJ in 2019. Similarly, the household sector consumed 48102 TJ of RE, which increased to 50070 TJ in 2019. The consumption of RE by other sectors, including agriculture, also increased from 725 TJ in 2014 to 2112 TJ in 2019. Electricity in Bhutan is generated by RE sources in entirety. In 2020, it generated 11371 GWh of electricity through hydro and marine power. In 2014, Bhutan imported 8386 TJ of energy, which increased to 9558 TJ in 2019. Energy exports from the country in 2014 were 19218 TJ, which witnessed a rise to 22781 TJ in 2019 (IRENA, 2022b).

Bhutan has not diversified its energy basket and has limited itself to hydropower given its clean energy credentials and economic advantages. Bhutan exports over 70 per cent of its hydroelectricity to India, contributing significantly to its GDP. Hydropower, as a form of clean energy, has enabled Bhutan to have a carbon negative growth, and it continues to seek financial and technical assistance for sustainable development, aiming to generate 10,000 MW of hydropower and 1,000 MW of solar energy by 2035 and 2030, respectively (Confederation of Indian Industries, 2023). This also sits well with its philosophy of Gross National Happiness, which emphasises environmental conservation and sustainable economic development (Dorji, 2016).

India

India is currently the third largest country in the world for electricity generation after China and the United States (US). As of April 2023, the total installed generation capacity of India was 416351 MW (Ministry of Power, Government of India, 2022). With rapid industrialisation and urbanisation and improved standards of living of Indian households, the power demand in the country, the world's sixth largest economy, is likely to grow significantly (*Business Insider Bureau*, 2023). Eighty-one per cent of the electricity is generated through non-renewable sources while the rest is generated from RE sources

(10 per cent from hydro and marine; 3 per cent from solar; 4 per cent from wind; and 1 per cent from geothermal).

Ninety-nine per cent of India's population had access to electricity in 2020. The TFEC from RE sources in 2020 was 33 per cent. The total energy supply in 2019 was 40573062 TJ, which increased from 33677646 TJ in 2014. Of this, the share of non-renewable sources far exceeded that of the RE sources. The share of non-renewables in the total energy supply in 2014 was 26245320 TJ, which increased to 31716684 TJ in 2019. The share of RE in total energy supply in 2014 was 7432326 TJ, which increased to 8856378 TJ in 2019. Renewables constituted 22 per cent of the total energy supply, while the rest comprised coal (47 per cent), oil (24 per cent), gas (6 per cent), and nuclear energy (1 per cent). The major share of RE in 2019 was that of bioenergy (89 per cent), and the rest included hydro and marine (6 per cent), wind (3 per cent), and solar (2 per cent). Thus, coal has underpinned the expansion of electricity generation and industry and remains the largest single fuel in the energy mix. In 2014, India imported 15056785 TJ of energy, which increased to 19411206 TJ in 2019. Energy exports from the country in 2014 were 2732057 TJ, which witnessed a rise to 3004596 TJ in 2019 (IRENA, 2022c).

According to the International Energy Agency (2021), the total energy production in India in 1990 was 10675 TJ, which rose to 23780 TJ in 2020. The RE consumption in the country has also witnessed an increase across sectors. The residential sector consumes the maximum RE at 57 per cent, followed by industries at 38 per cent, and others, including transport and agriculture, at 5 per cent (IRENA, 2022c). India's installed generation capacity from non-renewable sources is 2,37,269 MW, while from RE, it is 172,542 MW. India has 46850 MW of hydropower installed generation capacity, and from wind, solar, and other RE sources, it generates 125,692 MW of energy (Ministry of Power, Government of India, 2023).

Nepal

The energy sector is seen as a pivotal element for Nepal's future inclusive economic growth and the achievement of its development goals, as outlined in government policy documents (Nepal Energy Efficiency Programme, 2024). The Constitution of Nepal (2015) designates the hydro energy sector as a crucial component of its poverty reduction and economic growth strategy. Article 51 (g) (3) states, "To ensure a reliable supply of energy in an affordable and easy manner, and make proper use of energy, for the fulfilment of the basic needs of citizens, by generating and developing renewable energy" (Constitution of Nepal, 2015). In line with the new Constitution, the government has prepared a roadmap to develop the hydroelectric sector by inviting investments, encouraging private sector participation, and negotiating with neighbouring countries to export surplus energy.

The total energy production in Nepal has risen from 230 TJ in 1990 to 453.43 TJ in 2019 (IEA, 2023). The TFEC from RE sources in 2020 was 77%. The total energy supply in 2019 was 598140 TJ, which increased from 542902 TJ in 2014. Of this, the share of RE sources far exceeded that of the non-renewable sources. The share of non-renewables in the total energy supply in 2014 was 86748 TJ, which increased to 135023 TJ in 2019. The share of RE sources in the total energy supply in 2014 was 456155 TJ, which increased to 463117 TJ in 2019. The RE consumption in the country has also witnessed an increase across sectors.

The residential sector consumes the maximum RE at 93 per cent, followed by industries at 5 per cent, and others, including transport and agriculture, at 2 per cent. Nepal's installed generation capacity is from RE sources. Hydro and marine constitute 95 per cent of the total capacity, while the rest is from solar and others. Non-renewable energy sources do not have any contribution (IRENA, 2022d).

The country expects domestic demand to increase to nearly 6,000 MW by 2030, thereby necessitating an investment of almost $6.45 billion in downstream infrastructure. Since the Hindu Kush Himalayan region remains vulnerable to climate change, it is important for the governments of Nepal and India to work together in association with the private sector developers and the civil society for investments in new projects as well as for the maintenance of the existing HEPs.

Understanding the Hydropower Potential of Bangladesh, Bhutan, and Nepal

Hydro-Diplomacy

Hydro-diplomacy refers to an emerging concept and a practical approach built on the debates surrounding the issues of environmental security, conflict, cooperation, and the need for peace that gained momentum at the end of the Cold War (Farnum, 2018). While hydro-diplomacy facilitates communication between sovereign states to establish relationships to (re)build trust that helps prevent further water conflicts, yet the whole process is highly formal and state-driven, often leaving deliberations in a stalemate and pervasive mistrust between states (Barua and Vij, 2018). It remains to be biased towards natural scientists and systematically overlooks the contributions of the social scientists in demonstrating the significance of institutions, institutional actors, culture and identity debates, foreign policy, and security debates (Pohl & Swain, 2017).

In this light, hydro-diplomacy between the BBIN states has remained less than optimal. While in the recent past, a few Track II and Track III cooperation initiatives have taken place, led by non-state actors, involving bilateral and multilateral discussions (Barua, 2018), and multilateral funding agencies, like the World Bank, the ADB and others, have endeavoured to establish varied benefit-sharing arrangements involving communities and other stakeholders in the transboundary waters of South Asia (Hanasz, 2017), yet such approaches have witnessed low to marginal success. This is primarily attributed to their short-term funding cycles and an overall lack of interest of the governments to sustain such joint mechanisms (Uprety and Salman, 2011; Hanasz, 2017).

Hence, it has been asserted that the governments of the region must undertake a proactive stance, which would lead to developing strategic cooperation for optimum exploitation and sharing of energy resources, and simultaneously encourage multi-track diplomacy to recognise the plurality associated with transboundary waters, acknowledging and streamlining the power asymmetry among the riparian countries, highlighting the significance of the principles of international water laws and their relevance in the BBIN for guiding hydro-diplomacy, and paving the way for an effective science-media communication that would enable the shaping of narratives around transboundary waters for the people of the sub-region (Hazarika et al., 2023).

The importance of multi-stakeholder participation in hydro-diplomacy lies in the varied ways a transboundary water body is perceived: physical (the water that can be seen and felt), mental (the water that involves a consideration of its efficiency or price), emotional (water resource that involves politics of power, sovereignty, and equity), and spiritual (water which is inextricably tied to traditions and faith) (Porta & Wolf, 2021). Involving only the technicalities of hydro-diplomacy runs the risk of focusing on the physical and mental waters (given the measurability of water) and ignoring the emotional and spiritual waters. This implies that due to the neglect of the emotional and spiritual waters, inter-state conflicts arise. Hence, Track II and Track III hydro-diplomacy would bring in the civil society and grass-roots organisations that would be instrumental in negotiating national egos and critical disputes (Wolf and Shubber, 2020). A multi-stakeholder participation in hydro-diplomacy in BBIN becomes all the more important because of rising demand for energy in the sub-region along with the precarity caused by a changing climate. Hence, as a low-carbon energy source with great development potential, hydropower would have a significant role in this situation. It remains a matter of great opportunity and optimism that India's neighbours in the sub-region have huge potential in hydroelectricity, and cooperation among them to tap the energy resource is poised to be a win–win situation for all.

In all this, the importance of private sector participation cannot be underrated. The 1990s heralded the era of liberalisation, privatisation, and globalisation throughout the South Asian countries, but the phenomena were under-harnessed when it came to private sector cooperation between countries. Hence, the sub-regional cooperation framework has espoused cooperation for the development of the private sector, development of regional communication infrastructure, and equity in development cooperation. This is especially true for hydropower development in the Sustainable Development Goal (SDG) era, with investors and developers from the private sector taking on an increasingly prominent role in realising projects (Merme et al., 2014), where such investment in renewable energy technologies may contribute to achieving the Goals, specifically, on ensuring access to affordable, reliable, sustainable, and modern energy (Goal 7) (Güney, 2019). The increasing role of the private sector therein is in line with broader trends in global development. Calls for more private sector leadership in progress towards global development targets have intensified in recent years (Scheyvens, 2016), with private and 'blended finance' being promoted as sources of development funding (Mawdsley, 2015).

In Bangladesh, due to chronic power shortages, over 80 per cent of the manufacturers are equipped with captive power, mostly gas- fired thermal engines. That is, there is redundant investment in Bangladesh by power companies and manufacturers, even though they are able to purchase fuel and natural gas inexpensively owing to the government's subsidy. The generation cost of such captive power is estimated to be 1.5 times higher than the usual grid's electricity tariff. This situation has obviously undermined the international competency of the manufacturers, leading to immense economic costs paid and obstacles of investment.

To overcome the above constraints and to fulfil Bangladesh's policy of "electricity to all by 2021", targeting the electrification rate of 100 per cent and 600 kwh per capita, Bangladesh's demand is forecasted at 33,000 MW in 2030. To meet the said forecasted demand, a long- term transmission plan has also been prepared in the country, taking into account the potential interconnection with neighbouring countries.

The Government of Bhutan aims to attract private investment for hydropower development in the country through independent power producers (IPP). Bhutan aims to provide sufficient incentives for investments in hydropower projects of the country and ensure sale of electricity outside the country by IPPs, thereby promoting regional trade (ADB, 2010; World Bank, 2007).

Bilateral cooperation

India-Bhutan

The government of Bhutan has widely acknowledged the role of India in enabling the country to harness its hydropower resources. India has been the lead donor in providing both technical and financial assistance to develop the numerous hydropower projects in Bhutan. Bhutan has a feasible hydro potential of 23,760 megawatts (MW) from 76 hydro schemes (greater than 10 MW capacity). Out of this, 2136 MW has been developed with Indian technical and financial assistance. Further, 2820 MW (11.86 per cent) is under construction and 6745 MW (28.39 per cent) is under various stages of development with Indian technical and financial assistance.

The relationship developed in the hydropower sector has been a win-win situation for both the countries. India has a huge power shortage while Bhutan has a large hydropower potential (Tshreing and Tamang, n.d.). Bhutan exports about 75 per cent of its total electricity generation. Annual electricity exports were about 7216.53 million units (MU) in 2010. Revenue from the sale of electricity contributes to 40 per cent of the national revenue. Thus, the electricity trade between Bhutan and India could be leveraged to bridge Bhutan's trade deficit with India (United Nations, 2013).

Bhutan's growth needs, which are dependent on hydropower generation and trade with India, ensure that the relationship is largely mutually beneficial. "Bilateral cooperation on water with India began in 1955 with the establishment of numerous rain gauges and river flow stations in Bhutan financed by the Indian Ministry of External Affairs for the purpose of improving flood warning measures" (Saklani et al., 2020).

India-Bhutan hydropower cooperation began with the signing of the Jaldhaka Hydel Power Project that began in 1961 and was commissioned in 1967 with a total installed capacity of 27 MW (Sharma, 2021). This was followed by the Chukha Hydroelectric Project (HEP) on Wangchhu (Raidak River) signed in 1974, Kurichhu HEP on Kurichhu signed in 1994, and Tala HEP on Wangchhu (Raidak River) signed in 1996. For India, there has always been a need to harness power sources to meet its ever-growing energy demands. Over the years, export of surplus power from these HEPs to India has funded many development initiatives in Bhutan, like the provision of free basic healthcare (Saklani and Tortajada, 2019).

While the framework of the above projects was derived from the Indo-Bhutan Friendship Agreement of 1949, the ongoing cooperation takes its cue from the 2006 Agreement on Cooperation in Hydropower and the 2009 Protocol to the 2006 agreement. Taking Indo-Bhutan cooperation further, India had agreed, under the 2009 protocol, to develop 10,000 MW of hydropower in Bhutan by 2020 and import surplus electricity. An Empowered Joint Group of Ministers, set up under the Protocol to the 2006 agreement with the aim of expediting hydropower project development in Bhutan, took this decision in its first meeting in March 2009 (Bisht, 2011).

Bhutan has expanded its economy by leveraging its hydropower potential, and the sector continues to remain highly profitable for the country (Dorji, 2016). The importance of the hydropower sector to Bhutan's economic growth was made clear when in 2018, growth slowed down to 3 per cent from the previous year's 4.7 per cent. This slowdown was attributed mostly to the decline in hydroelectricity production at Chukhha and Tala plants (owing to reduction in hydrological flows). In the year 2019, Bhutan's GDP grew at 5.5 per cent as compared to 3.1 per cent in 2018. The Annual Report for 2020 by the Royal Monetary Authority of Bhutan stated that: "The growth was largely contributed by the hydropower, and education and health sectors. The commissioning of the Mangdechhu hydropower project combined with favourable hydrological conditions supported the revival of the hydropower sector from negative 14.9 per cent in 2018 to 12.1 per cent in 2019" (RMA, 2020). It must be pointed out here that during the COVID-19 lockdowns, Bhutan's export of electricity to India reached a record high, earning Rs 27 billion in 2020 and INR 16 billion in 2021 due to it being a guaranteed market for Bhutan's excess electricity under the power purchase agreements (PPA) between Bhutan and India (Dorji, 2021; SASEC, 2022). The electricity generated from these projects is exported to India after meeting the internal demand of Bhutan through the Associated cross-border Transmission System (ATS). PTC has been identified as the nodal agency for the purchase and selling of imported power to India. All the power exported from Bhutan to India is under a long- term power purchase agreement. India also exports power to Bhutan during the winter season when there is a reduced hydrogeneration in Bhutan.

In the first phase of India-Bhutan hydro-cooperation till 2006, financial grants to Bhutan were accorded an important role. Almost all the projects during this phase—Chukha, Kurichhu, or Tala—had a 60 per cent grant component and 40 per cent loan component. Even the loans were provided at low interest rates due to Bhutan's economic condition and its need for support from India for economic growth. India had completely financed the first two five- year plans of Bhutan launched in 1961. Grants played a crucial role in reducing Bhutan's financial burden. The second phase of cooperation, from 2006 onwards, witnessed a shift in the financial modalities of the HEPs. India successfully pursued an increase in the loan component of financial assistance with a decrease in grants component (Premkumar, 2016). There were differences between the early projects of the second phase and those passed later. For Punatsangchhu-I, the grant to loan ratio became 40:60, and for Punatsangchhu-II, it further changed to 30:70. It is believed that these changes gradually contributed towards increasing the debt burden of the Bhutanese government. India continues to seek amendments in the financial arrangements of inter-governmental hydropower projects. In the latest round of negotiations on the Sunkosh project, India is pushing for a 20:80 arrangement. India's argument is that since Bhutan's economic condition has improved over the years, it makes sense to change the terms of financial assistance. India now views the projects through a more commercial lens, arguing that such an approach will bring greater accountability. There has also been an increase in the interest charged on the loan component in recent years. These changes have made India vulnerable to accusations of increasing conditionality and "undermining the interests of the Bhutanese state" (Saklani and Tortajada, 2016). However, there is also a view that such changes help Bhutan claim a greater and equal influence over the projects and become a stakeholder on equal terms.

Only a small proportion of Bhutan's hydropower potential has yet been developed. Potentially, Bhutan can be a large power exporter to neighbouring countries like India. With respect to India's Northeast region in particular, there is strong interdependence between the region's energy demands, India's clean energy goals, and Bhutan's hydropower sector.

India–Bhutan interconnection: For import of power from Bhutan, the following projects have been in operation Table 2.1 below:

Table 2.1: India-Bhutan Hydropower Cooperation

Name of HEP	River	Installed Capacity	Year of Commissioning
Jaldhaka	Jaldhaka, India	27 MW	1967
Chukha	Wangchu/Raidak, Bhutan	336 MW	1974
Khurichu	Khurichu, Bhutan	60 MW	1994
Tala	Wangchu/Raidak, Bhutan	1,020 MW	1996
Mangdechhu	Mangdechhu, Bhutan	720 MW	2019
Punatsangchu I	Punatsangchhu, Bhutan	1200 MW	2008
Punatsangchu II	Punatsangchhu, Bhutan	1020 MW	2023 (delayed due to the pandemic)
Sankosh	Sankosh, Bhutan	2585 MW	Negotiations between India and Bhutan are underway.

Source: Power Grid Corporation of India Limited.

India-Nepal

The Government of Nepal is giving priority to develop its vast hydropower reserves to meet its growing demand for energy and power export to India. The total energy production in Nepal has risen from 230 TJ in 1990 to 453.43 TJ in 2019 (IEA, 2023). Nepal has a huge exploitable hydropower potential of 44,000 MW. Large potential projects being considered for development and export of power to India have been shown in the following Table 2.2:

Table 2.2: India-Nepal Hydropower Cooperation

Name of HEP	River	Installed Capacity	Year of Commissioning
Upper Karnali	Karnali	900 MW	Proposed
Tamakoshi III	Tamakoshi	200 MW	Announced
Pancheshwar	Mahakali	Around 4800 MW	Proposed
Saptakoshi	Saptakoshi	3000 MW	Proposed
Arun- III	Arun	900 MW	2024
West Seti	Seti	750 MW	Announced in 2022
Lower Manang Marsyangdi	Marsyangdi	140 MW	2026
Upper Marsyagdi 2	Marsyangdi	327 MW	2028

Nepal is interconnected with India at various places through 11kV, 33kV, 132kV, and 220kV lines. The 1997 landmark agreement between India and Nepal allowed power trade of 150 MW between the two countries. Nepal and India are now working on three 400 KV D/C cross-border lines (Butal–Gorakhpur, Duhabi–Purnea and Dhalkebar–Muzaffarpur), which are in place but under a different model—the independent company model. Unlike inter-governmental exchange modalities, the new modality involves the establishment of two transmission companies, both in Nepal and in India, and these companies will develop these lines within their territories. The Dhalkebar–Muzaffarpur transmission line is an initiative to facilitate the development of transmission interconnection between India and Nepal for the mutual interest and benefit of both countries. It would import power from India in the initial years to reduce the power shortage in Nepal and, ultimately, export power to India when sufficient hydropower generation would develop in Nepal (Export-Import Bank of India, 2014).

A total of about 700 MW of power is being supplied to Nepal through these interconnections. Further, the 400kV D/C Gorakhpur (India)–Butwal (Nepal) line, 400kV D/C Dhalkebar (Nepal)–Sitamarhi (India) line, 132kV D/C Nanpara, Bihar (India)–Kohalpur (Nepal) line, and stringing of second circuit of 132kV line Kataiya (India)–Kushaha (Nepal) and 132 kV Raxaul (India)–Parwanipur (Nepal) lines have been agreed upon (Ministry of Power, Government of India, 2021).

The Nepal Electricity Authority (NEA) is the single buyer of electricity from IPPs for transmission and distribution. It concludes PPA agreements with IPPs as well as generates electricity on its own or through a subsidiary.

About 22 links at 132/33/11 KV have been identified. About 50 MW of power is being exchanged in radial mode, and supply of 70 MU/annum from Tanakpur (India) to Nepal (as per the Mahakali Agreement) is going on. About 10 per cent of Nepal's demand is met from India. It needs to be mentioned here that considering the water security issues of the riverine communities of the Mahakali River between India and Nepal, the Transboundary Rivers of South Asia (TROSA) project of OXFAM was instrumental in building a community consciousness in the Mahakali hydro diplomacy discourse (Bisht, 2019).

Muzaffarpur–Dhalkebar transmission line: It is one of the important transmission lines between Muzaffarpur (India) and Dhalkebar (Nepal) and is in progress. It is a 400 kV interconnection and its length is 125 km. The line length of the Indian portion is about 86.43 km, and the estimated cost is INR 131.75 crores. It is to be implemented by Cross Border Power Transmission Company Pvt. Ltd. (CPTC). The proposed equity shares of the joint venture's partners are IL&FS (38 per cent), Power grid (26 per cent), SJVNL (26 per cent), and NEA (10 per cent).

The line length of the Nepalese portion is 39 km, and the estimated cost is 131.75 crores. It is to be implemented by Power Transmission Company Nepal Ltd. (PTCN). The proposed equity shares of the joint venture's partners are NEA (50 per cent), Power grid (26 per cent), financial institutions of Nepal (14 per cent), and Infrastructure Leasing & Financial Services (IL&FS) (10 per cent).

In January 2024, India's External Affairs Minister visited Nepal and brought into effect PM Modi's initiation of importing 10,000 MW of electricity for a decade, during the then PM of Nepal, Pushpa Kamal Dahal's visit to India in June 2023 (*The Wire*, 2024; Ministry of External Affairs, 2023).

It is encouraging to witness the BBIN energy cooperation bearing fruit. On July 28, 2024, Nepal signed a tripartite power trading deal to export 40 MW of electricity to Bangladesh via India from June 15 to November 15 every year. The signatories to this Power Sales Agreement would comprise officials from the NEA, the Bangladesh Power Development Board (BPDB), and the NTPC Vidyut Vyapar Nigam Ltd (NVVN).

As per the agreement, Nepal will get a tariff of $0.064 per unit for selling electricity to Bangladesh. Nepal will transmit energy to India through the 400KV Dhalkebar-Muzaffarpur cross-border transmission line. India will then transmit the equivalent to Bangladesh. The delivery point will be a 400kV substation at Muzaffarpur in India, and Bangladesh will pay the transmission charge for using the Indian transmission infrastructure. According to an estimate by the NEA, Nepal will receive around Rs 330 million through the sale of electricity (*Deccan Herald*, 2024).

India-Bangladesh

Bangladesh has been trying to explore the possibilities of building electrical interconnections with neighbouring countries for a long time. A high capacity interconnection between India and Bangladesh exists through Baharampur (India) – Bheramara (Bangladesh) 400kV D/C lines along with a 2x500 MW HVDC back-to-back terminal at Bheramara. Another 400kV (operated at 132kV) interconnection exists between Surajmaninagar (Tripura) in India and Comilla in Bangladesh. These interconnections cumulatively facilitate transfer of power of the order of 1160 MW to Bangladesh (Ministry of Power, Government of India, 2021).

The potential interconnections are mentioned below:

1. *From Meghalaya, India*: It is considered that the new transmission line for the interconnection will be difficult due to geographical factors, though hydro potential exists.
2. *From Tripura, India*: Recently, large reserves of natural gas have been discovered in the Indian state of Tripura, which is adjacent to the east of Bangladesh; the Pallatana gas power generation project (726.6 MW) is planned. It is considered that the majority of the power generation will be consumed by the home country as the solution to power shortage, and a portion of the generation can be traded to Bangladesh. Power import of about 100 MW from Tripura has been discussed, and it is expected that the amount could increase in future. For this reason, the transmission infrastructure for grid interconnection is proposed to have the capacity of importing 500 MW, which is a 230 kV double circuit line from Tripura to Comilla. A synchronous connection with dedicated generating units is considered as a low cost solution instead of a back to back HVDC interconnection.
3. *From Assam, India*: There is potential for coal and hydropower in Assam. The reinforcement of the power system in India will be necessary because Assam is situated far from Bangladesh.

The expansion of the transmission network, including cross-border interconnections, as well as enhancement of power generation is mandatory to meet the future power demand growth, which requires huge investment. It is impossible for the government power sector to bear such huge investment alone. Hence, cooperation with other sectors, such as industry and commercial enterprises, will be needed for investment as private-public partnership (PPP) for successful implementation of the infrastructure.

India-Bangladesh interconnection: A MoU had been signed between an Indian delegation and officials of BPDB & PGCB on

November 24, 2009, at Dhaka. The Indian portion is being executed by Powergrid, India, while the Bangladesh portion is executed by Power Grid Company of Bangladesh Ltd. (PGCB), Bangladesh. The total cost estimated for the Indian portion is Rs 169.86 crores (USD 36.06 million), and for the Bangladesh portion, it is Rs. 736.84 crores (USD 156.44). The commissioning schedule is April 2013. The ADB extended about USD 100 million equivalent loans for India–Bangladesh cross border electricity interconnection to increase South Asia power trading (ADB, 2010). The transmission project for a new 415 km 765 kV D/C transmission line between Katihar and Parbotipur, under planning between Bangladesh and India, will result in almost 1,000 MW additional capacity.

Table 2.3: Major Energy Projects between India and Bangladesh

Energy Project Name	Type	Progress
Baharampur (India) - Bheramara (Bangladesh)	400 kV D/c line and 500 MW HVDC B/b station at Bheramara (Bangladesh)	Completed in 2013
Bangladesh (Parbatipur depot of the Bangladesh Petroleum Corporation (BPC)) -India (Siliguri Marketing Terminal of the Numaligarah Refinery Ltd (NRL)) Pipeline	129.5km refined petroleum pipeline	Under Construction
Suryamaninagar power sub-station in Agartala – Comilla in southern Bangladesh Transmission Line	400 KV electricity transmission line for transmission of 100 MW power from Tripura's 726 MW gas- based thermal power project at Palatana in Gomati district	Completed in 2016
Meghnaghat power station being developed through Reliance Power, a part of Reliance Group, that owns the project through its subsidiary, Reliance Bangladesh LNG, & Power Limited (RBLPL) on the banks of the Meghna River in Meghnaghat, Narayanganj district, Bangladesh	750 MW gas-fired power plant	Agreement signed in 2015

Rampal power plant, also known as Maitree super thermal power project, located approximately 14 km away from the Sundarbans at Moithara, Rampal, in Bagerhat district, approximately 23 km south-east of Khulna city, Bangladesh	1,320 MW coal-fired power plant	Part of the power plant started commercial production in December 2022. Second part of it is expected to start production in 2024.
Katihar (Bihar, India)-Parbatipur/ Barapukuria (Bangladesh)-Boranagar (Assam)Transmission Line	765 KV electricity transmission line	Under discussion and review for implementation

Unlocking the Potential for a BBIN Sub-Regional Power Grid

The natural complementary mix of energy generation resources in the BBIN sub-region makes the countries perfect partners for trade in electricity. Since all countries in the BBIN sub-region share a border with India, the latter is able to carry out CBET without requiring transit access through a third country. However, all other countries require transit access through India to trade with one another. The revised guidelines issued on December 18, 2018, made a provision for cross-border trade of electricity across India in Clause 3.1, which is a major breakthrough for regional power trade (Ministry of Power, Government of India, 2018).

While Nepal and Bhutan primarily have hydro-based power, which is seasonal and depends on water inflows, India and Bangladesh have majorly thermal-based power. India has coal-based and Bangladesh has oil and gas-based energy sources. There are times when the excess water from Nepal during the monsoons is wasted, which otherwise could be efficiently utilised in Bangladesh or India or both. Further, during the winter season, when Nepal's rivers have low inflow, the country suffers from power deficit. Understanding the gravity of this situation, India and Nepal signed a power agreement according to which the surplus electricity from Nepal during the monsoons, i.e., the wet season, can flow into India, and in the dry season, i.e., during the winters, the same quantum of electricity can be returned to Nepal from India. Besides, the other countries of the sub-region can also purchase RE from India in order to fulfil their NDCs. During times of uncertainties, Nepal and Bhutan can balance the demand through their capacities to quickly generate hydropower (Batra, 2020).

At the initial stage, it was to be a short-term buying and selling of power with Bangladesh, Nepal, and Bhutan, since India has grid connectivity with these countries. During his visit to Bangladesh, Indian Prime Minister Narendra Modi promised that power supply from India to Bangladesh would grow from 500 MW to 1100 MW within two years. The 1320 MW Rampal power project is making progress in accordance with Bangladesh's laws and regulation. 'The two countries can do more together in the power sector, in both Bangladesh and in India' (Ministry of External Affairs, Government of India, June 2015b). According to the former Indian High Commissioner to Bangladesh, Veena Sikri, power cooperation between India and Bangladesh is a 'unique example' and 'power-grid connectivity and the resultant energy cooperation between Bangladesh and India is set to scale new heights of success' (Sikri, 2015).

To enable more intra-regional electricity trade, including competitively-priced power generated from hydro-electric power projects in India, Nepal, and Bhutan, development of a 765kV Double Circuit cross-border electricity interconnection between Katihar (India), Parbotipur (Bangladesh), and Boranagar (India) was agreed upon in the India-Bangladesh Joint Statement during the official visit of the Prime Minister of Bangladesh to India (Ministry of Power, Government of India, 2021).

Given the ambitious capacity addition targets of the Indian government, the country's power market offers one of the highest growth opportunities for private developers. Further, under the current dispensation of PM Modi, a cross-border energy trade initiative is being pushed as part of the neighbourhood-first policy.

With the intent to build a South Asian energy security architecture, the Indian Energy Exchange (IEX), in April 2021, announced the "commencement of the Cross Border Electricity Trade (CBET)" on its platform (*Livemint*, 2021). A statement by IEX on CBET highlighted that this is a first-of-its kind initiative for the exchanges to expand their power markets beyond India to the South Asia region. This would facilitate the building of an integrated South Asian regional power market, where Nepal, Bangladesh, and Bhutan would be the first beneficiaries, owing to the connectivity with the Indian electricity grid. The proposed market, which will include these countries, could aid regional peace and improve utilisation of generation assets, including the stranded assets in India, with efficient pricing.

Nepal became the first country to avail the benefit of buying day-ahead power from power exchange through NVVN (NTPC Vidyut Vyapar Nigam Ltd). The policy thinking in India is that hydropower will provide a strong base to achieve India's clean energy transition goals by 2030 (*The Hindu*, 2021). This CBET will help the BBIN countries further. For instance, Nepal has the potential to earn significant revenue by selling its surplus hydro potential to India. This will correct its trade deficit with India and also bring in significant investments to develop its hydro infrastructure. Nepal also imports power from India to meet its domestic demand during the winter season when the hydro potential is low.

Participating in India's power market through CBET will also benefit Bangladesh, where the generation costs from heavy fuel oil (HFO), diesel, and naphtha can go as high as Taka 17 per unit. This can be optimally replaced with cheaper green power from India or other neighbouring countries, procured through India's spot markets. Over time, this can reduce Bangladesh's reliance on fossil fuels, helping the country meet its RE commitments, while optimising power costs.

Bhutan has significant hydropower and exports power to utilities in India. It, however, imports power from India during the lean hydro season. Currently, Bhutan exports 70 per cent of the total power generation to India (Goel, 2023).

The formal introduction of cross-border trade of electricity in the Electricity Act of 2023 has opened doors for a wider alliance between India and its neighbours for electricity trading. This is one of the most positive inputs towards Indian Prime Minister Narendra Modi's vision for One World, One Grid. Through this Act, not only all the BBIN nations will benefit, it will also lead to a broader integration of the entire world for efficient global power utilisation. India's stature as a responsible country towards sustainable development is set to be consolidated further, and hence, would be a geopolitical gain as well (Batra, 2020).

Currently, the cross- border trade with neighbouring countries for India stands at about 18 BU (billion units), conducted through medium to long- term bilateral contracts. As per the Central Electricity Authority (CEA) and the Central Energy Regulatory Commission (CERC), as on date, India imports 8.7 BU from Bhutan and exports 2.37 BU and 7 BU to Nepal and Bangladesh, respectively. The power trade with these countries is expected to increase to about 40 BU by FY22 and 70 BU by FY 27 (IEX, 2021).

Bhutan and Nepal have huge hydropower potential. It provides a good opportunity for energy trade within the region to bridge the demand–supply gap. A prerequisite for electricity trading is the establishment of a regional power grid. This view was adopted as a priority in the South Asian Association for Regional Cooperation (SAARC) Declaration issued in January 2004. Countries like Nepal and Bangladesh can generate income for national economic development by selling hydropower while importing countries, such as India and Pakistan, can benefit by reducing the constraints on growth imposed by inadequate electricity supplies. There is a huge potential for cross-border hydropower exchanges due to varying seasonal and daily load curves. In summer, Bhutan and Nepal usually have surplus power, and Bangladesh can import power from these countries to meet its high domestic demand. The under construction Dhalkebar-Muzaffarpur cross-country transmission line between India and Nepal can potentially provide the impetus for sub-regional cooperation between India, Nepal, Bhutan, and Bangladesh.

Due to its geographical location, India can benefit from the wheeling charges for the utilisation of its transmission system for power wheeling between these countries. India could provide transit rights for building dedicated transmission systems for power trading in the subcontinent. Power exchanges between India and Pakistan could also meet the demand of electricity in the border areas. Power exchange between India and Bangladesh is also possible, as suggested by the 'Regional Report' issued by the South Asia Regional Initiative for Energy Integration (SARI/EI). India's power generation in the eastern region can benefit Bangladesh's western region, and Bangladesh can supply power to India's north-eastern region. Such arrangements would reduce investment requirements, lower transmission losses, improve reserve margin, and enhance the reliability of supply.

The sub-regional energy trade would help overcome the mismatch between energy demand and energy resource endowments among the countries in the region. The overall energy security would be enhanced through prudent reliance on trade to meet part of the demand by diversifying the forms of energy access and supply sources with possible lowering of the average cost of supply. It clearly enables the smaller countries, especially Bhutan and Nepal, with large natural resources (such as hydropower) to develop that resource, exploiting economies of scale. Energy trade cooperation promotes public-private partnership arrangements. This enhances private sector participation in the energy sector, thereby maintaining competitiveness in the prices. Further, environmental benefits would be attained by enabling the substitution of planned higher per electricity unit pollutant emission projects in one power grid with lower per electricity unit pollutant emission projects in an interconnected power grid.

Field Visits to Nepal and Bangladesh (in 2022 and 2023, respectively)

Field visits were undertaken to Kathmandu (Nepal) in June 2022 and to Dhaka (Bangladesh) in January 2023 for five and three days, respectively. Meetings were organised with government functionaries, private energy producers, academic experts, and think tank officials.

In Kathmandu, the respondents highlighted several important viewpoints, which have a direct and indirect bearing upon the nation's energy potential. A summary of the same is provided below. They highlighted the need to reform Nepal's hydropower policies and bureaucracy at the national level; the need to mobilise funds for hydropower development from national, international, and multilateral sources; and most importantly, the need to advance the integration of Nepal's energy grid with those of its South Asian neighbours—particularly in the BBIN sub-region.

There was an unequivocal call to prioritise hydropower development in Nepal, for which the country needs to focus its efforts on reforming hydropower policy and bureaucracy at the national level. This is because, oftentimes, politics, bureaucracy, and policy uncertainty stand in the way of domestic and foreign investments in hydropower. A managing director at a private energy firm sounded the alarm that Nepal's regulatory system was hugely regulatory, leading to rent-seeking and corruption; the need of the hour was a regulatory system that works without licences. He commented that there are "too many things on paper that are not executed in reality", thereby acting as a roadblock to potential private investors.

A veteran scholar, earlier with Tribhuvan University, mentioned that political unrest in the past had deterred investments, since there was no access to hilly areas. Another respondent cited the recent establishment of a new national Electricity Regulatory Commission in December 2017, after two decades of efforts, as a positive indicator and opined that the greater political stability in recent years has proved to be a positive development in the regulatory context for hydropower investment. It maintains a balance between the demand and supply of electricity by making the generation of electricity, transmission, distribution, or business simplified, regular, systematic, and transparent, regulates the electricity tariff, protects the right and interest of the electricity consumers, and makes the electricity services reliable, available to all, qualitative, and secured. Further, it seeks to ensure consistency in the grid linked to the transnational distribution system and the grid of the international level.

Some respondents from the academic circle, who having had their education in India were easy on Indian investments, were vocal in their strong rejection of Chinese involvement in Nepali hydropower development. The scepticism with China was particularly due to cultural and political differences, where the private sector is not accustomed to operating in a democratic institutional environment, making them less desirable partners for Nepal. The business case for Indian and Chinese investors differed. Respondents reported that Indian investors still had many investment opportunities in their own country, making Nepal an unattractive destination for them. They also felt that market dynamics would override political concerns. The Chinese, in turn, were seen as somewhat more willing to take risks, since they receive governmental incentives to invest abroad, have a superior production chain for turbines and other hydropower- related engineering products, while also having exhausted most domestic opportunities for hydropower projects. Government functionaries put up a non-biased response to both Chinese and Indian investments. They welcomed the idea of investment in cross-border transmission lines in the BBIN region. The respondents prioritised the integration of Nepal's hydropower production with the South Asian energy market, calling for investment in cross-border transmission lines with the BBIN region as well as more stable demand from neighbouring countries, mainly India and Bangladesh, since Bhutan is already a net exporter of hydropower to India. They felt that this could be to the advantage of all BBIN countries. In this, the strategic calculus of India was seen to be most important. However, the impact of Nepal's experience of an economic blockade by India in 2015 was negative in the minds of the Nepalese and undermined trust in Indian entities as partners. Therefore, they highlighted the need for efforts at the national Nepali level rather than counting on support from abroad. They also supported investment in cross-border transmission lines in the BBIN region as a strategy to expand the market for Nepal's energy, with one respondent detailing Bangladesh's very high energy costs, which make exports from Nepal financially viable and beneficial to both countries.

The benefits of multilateral energy trading were recognised by all respondents. In fact, it was highlighted that technical challenges as well as political conflicts would be ironed out in view of the benefits accruing from the energy integration. One senior expert cited the integration of European countries' energy grids as a positive example, which could serve as a model for the energy future of South Asia.

Connecting hydropower development with geopolitics was not welcomed by most of the respondents. They mentioned that any source of funding was welcome, and that one country must not be favoured over another. However, a China-Nepal electricity grid was seen to be near to impossible, given the difficult mountainous terrain. This is much easier, as demonstrated by existing projects, in the case of India and Nepal. Therefore, it was recognised that Nepal strongly depends on India for energy trade along with third countries (notably, Bangladesh), making India Nepal's most important partner country, ahead of China, especially due to the geographical proximity, which meant lower transmission costs, and the strong cultural affinity between the two countries. The absence of visa restrictions for Indians was seen as another strategic advantage, meaning that the integration of energy grids needed to start with India.

The respondents, however, admitted that Nepal had understood from decades of experience as a recipient of Northern and Southern development assistance that power lies with those who control financial resources (Sharma, 2017). Therefore, in the long run, it was better for Nepal to build a more equal relationship with its partners and engage in mutually beneficial relationships. Nepal's reliance on imported fuels from its neighbouring country, India, has also made it highly vulnerable to international price fluctuations, and, as a landlocked nation, to foreign trade policy and sudden geopolitical shifts.

As regards multilateral and other funders from the developed world, the government officials saw them as providers of subsidised capital and technical expertise on a long-term basis, since Nepal does not produce any electro-mechanical equipment of its own. Some envisioned them as builders of dams with large reservoirs, which were seen as too costly for private investors from Nepal.

The private sector espoused their role in dam construction, with one developer mentioning that risk- taking ability rests with the private players, and they are always willing to invest for long- term gains in hydropower projects. Lastly, competitive bidding for power purchase agreements (PPAs) was strongly advocated to enhance efficiencies in the domestic energy trade, while the inefficiencies of the monopolistic administration of hydropower by the Nepal Electricity Authority (NEA) was criticised. It needs to be highlighted here that the Nepalese government ordered the NEA to sign power purchase agreements with the developers of run-of-the-river hydropower projects to undertake or pay modality for up to 1,500MW in February 2023 (*The Kathmandu Post*, 2023). The NEA had assumed a monopolistic position in Nepal's energy market through its formal and informal power networks (Pasanen et al., 2016).

All the respondents, except for the officials from think tanks and civil society, assigned the lowest priorities to climate change and the benefits that hydropower would bring to address it. One government functionary, in fact, stated that Nepal was too small a country to make a significant difference on global climate change and rather, melting glaciers would help the country.

NEA was heavily criticised for enabling unfair competition through negotiating more favourable PPA rates from its subsidiary companies as compared to IPPs (Rai et al., 2019) and resisting attempts to improve efficiency, despite sufficient pressure from donors and the government. Dominant discourses informed by geopolitical considerations, resource constraints, and external influences often override Nepal's domestic energy politics, leading to a skewed representation of views in Nepal's contemporary energy debates among academicians and policy-makers. In essence, some specific issues that need to be resolved to unlock Nepal's hydropower potential, as highlighted by the respondents from academia, include:

- amending the Electricity Act,
- reforming the NEA,
- setting up bilateral mechanisms between the power ministries of Nepal and neighbours,
- finalising the terms of PPAs and project development agreements, and
- designing fair risk-sharing arrangements between public and private sector (IFC, 2023).

Experts from Bangladesh emphasised the need to establish a framework agreement for energy cooperation. They also proposed the formation of a cross-border steering committee to promote multilateral dialogue on energy connectivity, provide financial assistance, and create a common platform for knowledge exchange to ensure energy security and comprehensive sustainable development in the region. A senior scholar at one of the country's think tanks highlighted the critical role of energy in sustaining BBIN's rapid economic growth, emphasising the importance of an uninterrupted energy supply to maintain this momentum. Acknowledging the energy security challenges in densely populated

South Asia, he underscored the need for cross-border cooperation. He also stressed that ensuring energy security without addressing climate change will not achieve the desired outcomes, pointing out the environmental costs of power trade.

In India, interviews were conducted, both offline as well as online, through Zoom. Experts included officials from the Ministry of Power, Ministry of New and Renewable Energy (MNRE), think tanks focusing on energy and environment, as well as the private sector energy companies.

The major challenges for the country in the slow pace of BBIN energy cooperation, as listed by the experts, included those posed by a rapidly expanding population in India and its repercussions on the economy, which is proving to be an impediment in securing a consistent, trustworthy, and economical energy cooperation provision. Added to this is the frequent disruptions caused by geopolitical pressures upon the cross-border transmission and grid integration, as a result of which the establishment of resilient transmission infrastructure and regulatory structures to facilitate efficient cross-border electricity exchange becomes difficult. Further exacerbating the challenges is climate change, which brings forth the significance of sustainable and eco-friendly energy alternatives as indispensable. Respondents from the private sector highlighted the urgent need for the government and agencies to co-opt them in the advancement of the power sector to foster mutual economic progress for BBIN energy cooperation.

Respondents from the Ministry of Power underscored the delicate balance needed between meeting domestic energy demand and leveraging the region's plentiful renewable resources. With the mission to provide reliable and affordable power to all the citizens of the sub-region, they advocated for the need for collaborative efforts, including the interconnectedness of electric grids to share resources and enhance energy security across the region, framework agreements, cross-border committees, and financial assistance between the member states to foster regional growth and prosperity. They expressed their apprehensions about the neighbouring states' lasting commitments in moving forward with any agreement, given the role that domestic politics play in their respective countries. Hence, to win the confidence of the investors—whether from the governments or from the IFIs or from the private sector—what is imperative is that stable policies must underscore the long- term development plans. Furthermore, the respondents from MNRE emphasised the integral role of hydropower and diverse renewable resources in the energy mix to ensure sustainable and clean energy solutions. The experts from think tanks advocated the need for a powerful regional grid, knowledge exchange platforms, and long-term agreements for cross-border power trade to foster regional unity and economic development that would withstand any domestic, regional, or global disruptions. To connect energy supply across borders, PM Modi's initiative of 'One Sun, One World, One Grid' under the ISA would be instrumental in facilitating efficient energy transmission.

Field work to Bhutan could not be conducted due to shortage of funding. However, online meetings with start-up entrepreneurs in the power sector were conducted. The literature on Bhutan's energy challenges and prospects corroborated with the online interviews. They emphasised Bhutan's substantial hydropower potential and noted the need to tap into this resource for the mutual benefit of the BBIN sub-region, in particular. For this, they favoured a common platform to address shared challenges and unlock the full potential of cross-border power trading.

Highlighting the seasonal variation in energy production due to the Himalayan winter, one professor at the College of Natural Resources at the Royal University of Bhutan pointed out the existing symbiotic relationship in energy consumption among the BBIN countries. However, he underscored challenges arising from transmission issues, seasonality, and the absence of a common platform for addressing energy-related problems. Advocating for regional cooperation, he called for transparent mechanisms for distributing transmission charges and the establishment of a common transmission access pricing mechanism.

This approach would enable multilateral trade by thorough utilisation of available transmission capacity. He further recommended the creation of a common regional energy exchange, fostering a shared marketplace for power trade. Drawing attention to Bhutan's winter energy deficit, he highlighted the importance of cross-regional energy supply solutions, emphasising the Indo-Bhutan relationship as a model for bilateral cooperation. Requirements for financial and technical support were unequivocally raised by the respondents, and they urged India to continue to remain at the forefront of it.

Having understood the different areas of energy cooperation amongst the BBIN countries and the prospects for the future, we must remember that nations are sovereign entities and always keep their national interests at the forefront. The next chapter (Chapter 4) discusses the various challenges that plague energy cooperation in the BBIN region, and the following chapter (Chapter 5) provides policy recommendations.

4

Challenges to Energy Cooperation at the Regional and Sub-Regional Level

This chapter makes unbiased assessments of energy cooperation within the BBIN sub-region, drawing on an extensive review of literature and data from both official and secondary sources. It intends to serve as a logical conduit for recommending appropriate policy measures to enhance the objectives of strengthening energy cooperation among these nations.

Bolstered by political will, the sub-region of Bangladesh, Bhutan, India, and Nepal (BBIN) forms a formidable, contiguous entity with enormous potential for forging an alternative approach to quadrilateral cooperation. The historical ties, geographical proximity, and ecological unity of this sub-region further reinforce the case for regionalism. Initially referred to as the South Asian Growth Quadrangle (SAGQ), the primary task of BBIN was to improve cross-border connectivity, stimulate trade, and bolster sub-regional economic integration.

However, political challenges arguably present the most significant hurdle to the realisation of regional energy projects in South Asia. This issue has inhibited cooperation despite the substantial economic incentives that exist. The BBIN initiative was initially met with reservations from the Maldives, Pakistan, and Sri Lanka. Pakistan viewed it as an attempt at isolation, while the Maldives and Sri Lanka also expressed serious concerns before eventually agreeing to it. The objectives, principles, and action plan for BBIN were agreed upon by the Foreign Secretaries of SAARC in April 1997. They identified six specific sectors—multi-modal transport and communications, energy, trade and investment facilitation, tourism, utilisation of natural resources endowment, and environment (Michael, 2013).

Regrettably, the initiative soon became a point of contention in the domestic politics of Bangladesh and Nepal. The main opposition parties—the Bangladesh Nationalist Party and the United Marxist Leninist Party—criticised their respective ruling governments for neglecting the interests of the people (Ali, 2014). As a result, the SAGQ failed to overcome the initial obstacles and succumbed to the internal politics of these two crucial member states. Despite these setbacks, the concept of facilitating economic cooperation has remained relevant since then (Shukla, 2019).

These challenges have hindered the realisation of energy projects. Security concerns have overshadowed pipeline proposals in the west, while concerns of hegemonic exploitation have stagnated hydroelectric projects in the east. Adding to this, New Delhi's insistence on the inclusion of Article X in the SAARC Charter has compounded the issue. This article enshrines the principle of unanimity in decision-making and excludes all bilateral and contentious issues from discussions. These two provisions have limited the decision-making powers of SAARC and effectively prevented the discussion of critical bilateral issues, perpetuating conflicts and thereby impinging on regional cooperation.

It should be noted that stimulating growth is not automatic; it requires a push. This impetus for the SAGQ could be provided by substantial investments in production and infrastructure development, which would catalyse further dynamism in the production sector. An opportunity for this sub-regional grouping lay in the hydropower production potential, where an estimated 40,000 MW remained unutilised, compared to the projected demand of around 33,000 MW by 2010 (Chattopadhyay, 1997). Therefore, it was maintained that, with cooperation in the energy sectors, the sub-region would never face an energy crisis.

When it comes to institutional improvements, it is essential to acknowledge that energy markets in individual South Asian countries are governed by separate legal, regulatory, and policy frameworks. The legal and regulatory risks multiply when cross-border energy transactions, which often have to recover high-cost, state-of-the-art technology investments, must contend with multiple energy sector legal and regulatory frameworks. The immaturity of these frameworks in individual countries and a lack of harmony among the rules and procedures necessary to facilitate cross-border energy trade and simplify transaction mechanisms represent constraints to energy trade. Therefore, SAARC members need to collaborate to harmonise their legal and regulatory frameworks, starting with regional electricity trade.

Most South Asian countries already have an institutional structure in place, with relevant energy ministries and energy sub-sector institutions. This facilitates the harmonisation of relevant energy sector frameworks within the region. The majority of South Asian countries have energy sector regulators. For example, while India has separate energy sub-sector regulators, Bangladesh has a single regulator for the entire energy sector. Such divergence in the mandate of regulators across the region may create coordination issues, but it is not expected to be a major impediment to the process of legal and regulatory framework harmonisation.

Financing large hydropower projects in the private sector faces inherent complexities due to complicated hydrological, environmental, and social issues. These challenges are distinct from those encountered in large thermal power projects, which primarily involve fuel conversion to produce specified electricity outputs while adhering to environmental standards. Given these complexities, catalytic funds (both equity and loans) and guarantee instruments are available to facilitate the financing of hydropower development from the private sector windows of multilateral financing institutions, such as the ADB. Nonetheless, it is vital to establish an enabling framework to encourage private sector participation. This framework should include internationally accepted measures to ensure the security of energy sector infrastructure and provide agreements relating to the return on these investments.

Political leaders within the domestic sphere have so far struggled to synchronise their objectives with regional cooperation. This has, in many ways, obstructed consensus- building on energy projects. The actions and attitudes of domestic political parties in South Asian countries have significantly undermined the viability of multilateral energy projects. This lack of cooperation has led to costs associated with inaction in energy diplomacy. Since the mid-1970s, India has been a red herring in Bangladesh, and political parties often resort to India-bashing to shore up their domestic constituency and win electoral gains. Gas exports from Bangladesh have become a politically sensitive issue, not so much as a commodity, but because who were to be the potential buyers (Kumaraswamy and Datta, 2006). The rivalry between the two major political parties, the Awami League (AL) and the Bangladesh Nationalist Party (BNP), resulted in a highly politicised and unrepresentative foreign policy, lacking national consensus or consideration of national interests. This situation has proven to be a significant obstacle to the realisation of regional energy projects.

During periods governed by the BNP, the bilateral relationship with India has tended to be tense, while under the AL-led government, relations have improved to such an extent that some observers have labelled them as sycophantic. Any attempt by a given administration to undertake energy cooperation with India is likely to face criticism from the opposition. Such extreme swings do not serve the interests of the country or the region in the long term.

In Nepal, the consistent political instability ensuing from a decade-long civil war that concluded in 2006 has significantly undermined the country's capacity to undertake regional cooperation. Constant feuding among Nepal's most prominent political parties—the Communist Party of Nepal-Maoists (CPN-M), the Unified Marxist- Leninist (UML), and the Nepali Congress (NC)—stymied the drafting of a constitution until September 2015. This political instability has hindered the Nepalese government from pursuing any initiatives towards regional energy cooperation. Mirroring the situation in Bangladesh, any cooperative endeavours with India are subject to political rhetoric in Nepal. Some extremist politicians in Nepal have propagated rumours and disinformation regarding bilateral projects with India. Electricity trade with India has been touted as "one more strategic weapon to the Indians against Nepal in their armory" (Shreshta, 2009). One of the reasons why Nepal has failed to exploit its hydroelectric resources is that energy has been politicised.

Certain constraints on expanding the scope of regional energy cooperation are rooted in the relationships between South Asian countries, which have been plagued by mistrust and a lack of transparency. These issues have, in turn, compounded poverty and deprivation in the region (Lama, 2007). This harmful mindset has substantially eroded goodwill and trust, leading to suspicion and doubt. The situation is further exacerbated by the failure of political leadership to sway public opinion towards developing a vision for regional cooperation, despite the existence of SAARC for over a decade. There is also a need for broader publicity at the national level regarding the rationale of energy trade policy and the sector reforms such a policy choice implies, to garner public support. The political commitment to energy trade, accompanied by the evolution of a consensus, facilitates the successful conclusion of trade deals. This approach is critically important in the case of Nepal and Bangladesh.

Even within India, the North-East region had been long overlooked, a trend which has noticeably reversed following the launch of the Act East Policy and several development projects initiated by the present Modi government. According to a retired Indian diplomat, in the years preceding 2014, India missed several opportunities to foster robust energy ties with neighbouring countries, such as Bangladesh, Bhutan, and Nepal.

While the Kingdom of Bhutan boasts greater political stability compared to its neighbours, its national discourse greatly emphasises environmental preservation. Consequently, Bhutan is unlikely to engage in regional cooperation at the expense of its environment, even if offered compensation. Bhutan's seclusion, combined with its commitment to the concept of Gross National Happiness, which positions the conservation of nature as one of its four pillars, places it at odds with countries like India and Bangladesh. These nations have pursued a more conventional development path, unlike Bhutan's culture of preserving its pristine natural environment, influenced by demographic and other reasons.

India's quasi-federal structure and the decentralised distribution of power make domestic actors in individual states significant players in regional negotiations. A divergence of objectives between the Union government and the states of India has also erected barriers concerning energy cooperation. Five states in India share an international border, and the role of domestic politics becomes especially powerful when negotiations involve neighbouring countries on issues such as water or energy. A notable example is the failure of the central government of India to reach an agreement with Bangladesh on the allocation of the Teesta River in 2011. This was due to opposition from the Chief Minister of West Bengal, Mamata Banerjee, who rejected the political implications that the agreement would carry in her constituency. Such attitudes often impede regional projects and lead to a deadlock.

Furthermore, India's consistent refusal to provide land access for Bangladesh to import electricity from Nepal and Bhutan through its territory has not only hampered multilateral cooperation in hydroelectricity but was also a key point of contention, leading to the shelving of the Myanmar-Bangladesh-India pipeline in 2005.

Apart from the aforementioned points, the role of influential foreign powers also significantly impacts the regional cohesion in India. For instance, China's Belt and Road Initiative (BRI) and String of Pearls strategy, aimed at influencing India's neighbours, creates instability within the domestic constituencies of these countries, which acts against regional cooperation. After the Myanmar-Bangladesh-India (MBI) pipeline was shelved due to unsuccessful negotiations between the three countries in 2005, China agreed to build a pipeline to import gas from Myanmar. Additionally, actions by the US and affiliated international donor agencies are often perceived as unsupportive of regional energy cooperation by some South Asian policymakers. They frequently suggest conspiracy theories that the US government is interested in establishing a regional energy market in South Asia because of the business opportunities such a market would offer US firms eager to sell electric equipment, a necessity for facilitating regional energy trade. A regional, homogeneous, and uniform market could potentially generate significant business opportunities for US companies. Some multinational corporations (MNCs) become entangled in exploitative practices when investing in regional energy projects, often encouraged by the domestic politics of the participating countries, which enable this kind of corruption.

In view of the enormous potential and benefits of promoting renewable energy, obstacles at both national and regional levels must be overcome. Among the notable challenges are the high initial capital costs involved in renewable energy and the fact that the monetary benefits from such projects take time to materialise. The following are challenges in renewable energy technologies:

Policy-wise Challenges

Negotiations for energy trading agreements are influenced by the unequal starting positions of the involved countries. Bangladesh and Nepal suffer from significant power shortages. Although India also faces energy shortages, it has an advantage due to its diverse energy sources, including pipelines, domestic coal, LNG imports, and domestic hydropower. Additionally, the concept of energy security varies among these nations. For Bangladesh and Nepal, energy security primarily means meeting domestic demand. However, Indian ministries also emphasise the importance of controlling energy generation sources. In Bhutan's case, India's strong influence over Bhutanese foreign policy and defence allows India to effectively control the security of its power supply from Bhutan. Such differing perspectives have led to several other policy challenges. These are:

- Lack of incentives for private sector involvement and inconsistent policies
- No feed-in tariff structure
- Fossil fuel subsidies
- Weak environmental regulations
- Low priority given to renewable energy in national planning and a weak implementation framework

Technical Challenges

While traditional challenges like grid compatibility, technological limitations, and knowledge coordination have historically made *de facto* export and import of energy difficult, the Bhutan-India model of power cooperation has shown that these obstacles are not impossible to be surmounted. Nonetheless, several technical constraints persist, with the two most significant being:

a. Grid synchronisation and grid codes: Currently, connections between Nepal and India operate in a radial mode with capacities of 13kV, limiting trade to border areas. This limitation also affects the very limited exchange between Bangladesh and India, as well as connections involving Bhutan, Nepal, and Bangladesh, with the "Chicken's Neck" of Indian territory obstructing any direct links.

b. Natural gas pipeline technology: Transmission lines are expensive to construct due to the investment in land rights, compensation for inhabitants, large compressors, and high-strength, large-diameter pipes. The passage of gas relies on computer modelling to manage extraction from storage just in time, avoiding the accumulation of unsold capacity in the pipeline. As gas is transported over long distances, strategically placed compressor stations maintain its pressure. Given the significant investment, pipeline companies aim to operate as close to maximum capacity as possible (Khosla, 2005). The investment costs and operating expenses of pipeline networks are so large that even small improvements in system utilisation can involve substantial amounts of capital (Ríos-Mercado and Borraz-Sánchez, 2015).

Apart from the above, the technical challenges that remain are:

- Limited technical capacity of nations to design, install, operate, manage, and maintain renewable-based modern energy services
- Technological constraints for reliable and comprehensive mapping
- Limited local manufacturing of specialised equipment
- Non-standardised technology

Economic Challenges

- Limited access to credit and insufficient government financial support
- Small economies of scale, high initial capital costs, and long payback periods
- Limited knowledge of market potential
- High installation costs at the end-user level
- High perceived risks and uncertainties

Information and Human Resource Challenges

- Limitations in a country's capacity for renewable energy (RE) data collection, analysis, and project development. There is a clear gap in communication between researchers and policymakers, with the latter often viewing the former's policy recommendations as antithetical to their current political office and future voting base. This, in turn, compromises the benefits that energy cooperation could offer.

- Insufficient information available on renewable energy and energy efficiency for policymaking and mobilising civil society.
- Insufficient expertise in business management and marketing skills. Lack of expertise and services in system design, installation, operation, and maintenance of renewable energy and energy efficiency technologies.

Additionally, resource nationalism exacerbates the difficulties in fostering healthy energy cooperation among the BBIN nations. Political leaders often prioritise the total resource value over the value of its benefits. For instance, certain political leaders in Bangladesh expressed scepticism when Indian companies signed production sharing contracts with Dhaka to explore hydrocarbons in the Bay of Bengal in early 2014. Political rhetoric about the total value of hydrocarbon deposits or hydroelectric potential in individual countries perpetuates the perception of energy resources as strategic assets that need control rather than ones that should be used for the betterment of humankind. In Bangladesh and Nepal, many commentators and some politicians are heavily opposed to electricity trade with India. They see it as "one more strategic weapon to the Indians against Nepal in their armoury" (Shreshta 2009). At the same time, politicisation of this issue is obstructing meaningful investment.

Listed below are the major challenges in the BBIN energy sector:

1. **Absence of a Competitive Power Market:** India is the only country in BBIN that has permitted electricity trade as a commodity and has recently established an energy exchange for electricity trading. Such options are not available to electricity buyers and sellers in other countries of the region. Although not a prerequisite for regional energy trade, a vibrant power market with competitive segments offers better opportunities for electricity trade.

2. **Lack of Funds:** Energy infrastructure, including power projects and transmission interconnections, require substantial capital outlay. BBIN countries lack sufficient financial resources for these projects' development and have to seek support from international donors and multilateral funding agencies.
3. **Non-existence of Harmonious Energy Policy and Related Framework:** Well-defined, coherent energy policies and an enabling legal and regulatory framework are essential for cross-border trade and investments (Ebinger, 2011). Thus, there is an urgent need for mechanisms that facilitate and encourage energy trade among the BBIN countries.
4. **Lack of Energy Infrastructure:** A prerequisite for energy availability is the existence of the requisite infrastructure to facilitate the transmission and transportation of energy supplies. The lack of infrastructure negatively impacts resource exploitation and access to available resources. Building robust energy infrastructure may reduce the need for dedicated transmission corridors across the region, and regional trade could be undertaken through interconnection points between neighbouring member states.
5. **Inadequate Infrastructure for Developing Remotely Located Hydro Projects:** Most hydropower projects are situated in remote and mountainous areas where infrastructures, such as accessible roads and high voltage transmission lines, are absent. This necessitates the development of these infrastructures for each project, with the associated costs being added to the overall project cost. This eventually leads to higher costs for the hydropower project, adversely affecting its competitiveness.
6. **Institutional Constraints:** Institutional barriers within the region impede the promotion of regional power exchange. The existing leadership has failed to advance the idea of power trade. No effective institutional arrangement exists among the other member countries of the region, except India and Bhutan, reflecting the priority given

by the member countries towards energy cooperation. A possible solution could start by identifying a focal institution in each of the member countries and setting up a network of these institutions responsible for working out an arrangement on energy cooperation (Srivastava and Mishra, 2007).

7. **Political Narratives:** Divergent national policies and political narratives of the governments in the region have proven to be a significant inhibitor of energy cooperation. Power trade should not be seen merely as a simple exchange of power but as a policy with the potential to bring about necessary changes in the equality, reliability, and efficiency of power supply, thereby accelerating economic growth (Lama,1999). Lama (2000), Gippner (2010), and Rana (2003) are among those academicians who have argued that sustained political will is crucial to the success of energy or any form of regional cooperation.
8. **Commercial and Financial Constraints:** Commercial barriers, in terms of tariffs, limit the ability to identify and evaluate the actual delivered cost of power. The central issue arises from the fact that power trading is most often treated based on political rather than commercial considerations (World Bank, 2007). Governments need to provide enabling agreements covering the sector, and the deal should be left to commercial decision-making to ensure its long-term sustainability and inject transparency and accountability.
9. **Lack of a Coherent and Efficient Power Sector:** The power sector in the region is predominantly state-owned. Despite power sector reforms, which envision a change in investment and ownership patterns, an increased role for private investment, a transformation of the power industry from the current single buyer model to a multiple buyer-multiple seller model, and the establishment of a strong and independent regulatory body, their implementation has been sluggish. Private sector involvement has been minimal, and poor financial performance of utilities has made them dependent

on scarce state funds, which face numerous other competitive claims. The slow progress in sector restructuring is recognised as an impediment to growth in the sector, both within the country and the region.

10. **Inefficient Operational Utilities:** Insolvency of utilities is another constraint to energy cooperation in trade and investment. Power systems in the region operate in a supply-constrained environment, with very low quality and reliability levels. Supply constraints in electricity trade have been highlighted by several scholars as one of the main energy governance challenges in ensuring security of supplies (Van de Graaf and Colgan, 2016; Brown et al., 2018). This involves disruptions and disputes related to cross-border pipelines and electricity grids and lack of transparent communication (Huda, 2022).

    Load shedding and power outages are common during peak hours and certain seasons. Electricity utilities are often used as vehicles of social policy, and average tariffs are kept substantially lower than supply costs. With such poor operational and financial performance, the entry of independent power producers for generation could only be possible based on a "take or pay" contract under full guarantee.

11. **Domestic political compulsions:** The political agenda of individual countries often create barriers to the realisation of energy projects among the BBIN member states. This indicates that the most pressing issue is not the relationship between the countries but addressing the concerns, well-being, and perceptions of local stakeholders where the energy project is constructed or implemented. Rumours about the entry of foreign countries and/or their companies can create widespread confusion, leading to protests and possibly stalling the project altogether.

12. **Different perspectives of environmental impacts of energy cooperation:** Discrepancies in perceptions of environmental impacts and security of trilateral hydroelectric projects between

the country producing the hydroelectricity and those importing it can pose a significant barrier to the realisation of projects between India, Nepal, and Bangladesh. Hydroelectric dams are considered economically and environmentally desirable in Bangladesh and India, with some policymakers referring to such projects as "clean and free of environmental harm". The Rampal Power Station, which is a coal-fired mega power plant being developed by India and Bangladesh near the Sundarbans, has garnered significant criticism due to its expected impact on the environment (Roy, 2023). Government officials from Nepal, while not undermining the economic benefits of hydroelectric projects, have highlighted the perceived negative impact of such ventures on the countries' environment. The civil society respondents and private sector representatives also conveyed their frustrations with India's unwillingness to compensate Nepal for losses due to flooding.

Building multipurpose hydroelectric power plants (HEPs) with large reservoirs disrupts river ecosystems and displaces human settlements and agricultural land. Additionally, the risk of water-borne contagious diseases in areas surrounding these HEPs is significant. While perceptions about these projects in Bangladesh and India are influenced by the desire to benefit from electricity import, Nepalese views are informed by the consideration that the actual construction of the dams would take place within their territory.

Barriers to a Renewable Energy Transition

This article discusses the primary barriers inhibiting the deployment of renewable energy technology. These obstacles can be broadly categorised into several key areas:

1. **Mobilising Investment, High Upfront Costs, and Uncertainty of Revenue Generation:** For renewable energy capacity to meet short-term targets and achieve India's long-term potential,

investment must gain momentum. This investment challenge involves addressing the higher upfront costs of renewables and the uncertainty of long-term revenue generation. Other associated issues include small economies of scale, high initial capital costs, and extended payback periods, as well as limited access to credit and insufficient government financial support. Moreover, there is limited knowledge about market potential, high installation costs at the user level, high perceived risks and uncertainties, and a lack of expertise and services in system design, installation, operation, and maintenance of renewable energy and energy efficiency technologies. The country's capacity for renewable energy data collection, analysis, and project development is limited. The shortage of employees trained in the skills needed to construct and operate decentralised renewable energy systems remains a continuing challenge and a barrier to meeting renewable energy targets. Additionally, there is a lack of quality information about renewable energy resources and technologies, efficient energy equipment suppliers, and potential financiers. Insufficient information available on renewable energy and energy efficiency for policy making, and a lack of mobilisation of civil society and business management and marketing expertise serve as additional roadblocks.

2. **Difficulties in the Business Environment**: Currently, the decentralised market is characterised by numerous different subsidies and standards, which are often neither monitored nor effectively implemented. Further, the lack of incentives for private sector involvement, inconsistent policies, an absence of feed-in tariff structure, low priority given to renewable energy in national planning, and a weak implementation framework all pose challenges. It needs to be recognised that private sector participation is crucial for the introduction and incorporation of new technologies and operating arrangements, as well as in improving the management and execution of projects in the energy sector. Investments from the

private sector reduce the financial burden on government budgets; hence, their importance cannot be underrated (Yépez et al., 2016).

3. **Bioenergy Challenges**: A pressing need exists to increase access to modern energy sources for hundreds of millions of India's people. Households consume nearly half of total energy in India, with around three-quarters consisting of traditional uses of bioenergy, which are both unhealthy and unsustainable. In contrast, modern bioenergy offers important socio-economic and human health benefits, particularly through efficient cookstoves.
4. **Required Solutions for Decentralised Energy Production and Storage**: India's grid infrastructure is already strained and needs significant improvements. Transmission and distribution losses are among the highest in the world, representing one-quarter of total electricity generation and even rising to two-thirds in some states. As the share of variable renewables (solar and wind) increases, the pressure will continue to mount on India's already stressed transmission and distribution grid. Integrating this growing variability will require more flexibility in power system infrastructure and storage. There is limited technical capacity to design, install, operate, manage, and maintain renewable energy-based modern energy services. Technological constraints exist for reliable and comprehensive mapping, limited local manufacturing of specialised equipment, and a lack of standardised technology.

To overcome the above challenges, it is important to strengthen existing and developing new national and regional institutions for investment in innovative energy infrastructure. Innovative and effective financing instruments, with appropriate incentives for the private sector, need to be developed. Furthermore, the support of multilateral and bilateral development institutions for new and effective assistance strategies that focus on innovative energy infrastructure investments cannot be underrated (Sarker, Hossain, and Islam, 2020).

The next chapter (Chapter 5) discusses the way forward in light of the challenges discussed here. It makes recommendations based on a thorough review and analysis of literature and field studies. Hence, the findings of this study are also of relevance to regional policymaking.

5

The Way Forward and Conclusions

Regional energy integration is a multifaceted concept that, despite facing challenges such as concerns over energy independence and sovereignty, offers considerable advantages. These benefits include (i) a reduction in wholesale electricity prices, (ii) a broader selection of energy suppliers for consumers, and (iii) enhanced infrastructure and cross-border trade in gas and electricity. By capitalising on the BBIN region's abundant yet unevenly distributed resources, particularly hydropower and natural gas, regional integration holds significant promise. However, realising this potential may take a long time, necessitating persistence and adaptability. Successful integration requires identifying the optimal level of integration, strategically investing on a regional scale, developing suitable regional institutions, achieving technical and regulatory harmonisation, reforming and integrating the power sector, and delineating the role of financial institutions.

The key prerequisites for advancing regional energy integration include (i) the long-term availability of electricity and gas from exporting nations in excess of their domestic needs, (ii) the harmonisation of regulatory frameworks for electricity and natural gas among countries, (iii) grid synchronisation to enhance transmission speed and volume, (iv) stable energy policies and regulations that attract both public and private investment, (v) active participation of both private and public sectors at different levels (Ramani, 2004), for instance, enhancing regional cooperation for sharing both "soft (knowledge, R&D, technology, etc.)

and hard (money and other physical resources) infrastructure" in the energy sector, (vi) a regional agreement ensuring that energy supplies via pipelines and transmission lines will not be capriciously interrupted, (vii) stable energy policies and regulations that attract both public and private investment, (viii) increasing the capacity at the national and sub-regional levels by improving governance and sharing knowledge and technology crucial to promote resource-centred strategies for enhancing energy security in the sub-region, and (ix) a long-term commitment to integration projects that outlast individual governmental tenures (Sarker, Hossain, and Islam, 2020).

While certain changes require long-term commitments to dialogue and understanding between states and populations in the region, the four nations need to address the mechanisms or practices that could advance regional cooperation on energy in South Asia. Such cooperation could ensure the long-term predictability and sustainability of energy provision and access in the region. If successful, it may stimulate or drive regional cooperation beyond energy issues. It should also help shift perceptions of energy security from a focus on sovereign control to one on availability and access. Thus, implementing energy cooperation within the geopolitical realities of the present puts the onus on the various political agents to reorient long-standing practices that have hindered cooperation.

The energy resource endowments among countries in the sub-region exhibit considerable diversity, especially in hydropower, natural gas, and coal resources. Nepal and Bhutan possess substantial hydropower potential that remains largely untapped. Conversely, coal resources are plentiful in eastern India, and natural gas reserves are found in Bangladesh. Additionally, the sub-region is rich in renewable energy sources, such as solar, wind, and biomass, which significantly contribute to meeting household energy demand. Nepal and Bhutan, being landlocked and devoid of significant fossil fuel reserves and production, depend entirely on India for fuel supply. Thus, the nature of the available resources, seasonal characteristics of electricity demand and hydropower generation, geographical proximity, and the political will within the sub-region create significant opportunities for power trading and fossil fuel supply (Gyanwali, 2020).

India currently enjoys substantial bilateral energy trade with all three of its bloc neighbours. However, transforming this bilateral energy trade into a potential for multilateral energy trade necessitates specific critical steps to build the right blocks. The Indian grid is viewed as a nucleus from which transmission infrastructure extends to meet the supply and demand needs of Bangladesh, Bhutan, and Nepal. The institutions that govern the grid, such as an independent national regulator, power traders, and spot markets, are viewed as assets that can be leveraged in the sub-regional power trade (Pillai and Prasai, 2021). Given the scale and potential of rural energisation programmes across all four countries, it becomes a significant proposition to enable smooth cross-border electricity trade. As India increasingly focuses on improving infrastructural capacities in the geographically rugged terrain of its North-East region, cross-border energy trade could help ensure the efficient and effective utilisation of locally available resources (Srivastava and Misra, 2007). Collecting data through mapping and information sharing is crucial to understanding the demand and supply drivers of energy in the sub-region (Ibid.).

Review of literature and interviews conducted have demonstrated the necessity of focusing on some basic, yet key components, to harness the energy resource endowments and potential of each of the BBIN nations. These can be summarised as: (a). need to set up effective and efficient institutions to deal with intra-sub-regional problems, (b). ensure government commitment to fairness and transparency, regardless of the regime, (c). establish clear planning of projects and selection criteria of funders, partners, and contractors, with the aim to reduce the construction and operating costs, (d). provide subsidies for capital costs, especially for RE projects, (e). charge fair prices from different segments of the population but not compromise on the long- term generation and supply costs, and (f). involve local communities to minimise friction and maximise benefits, especially in the case of HEPs.

International cooperation in renewable energy (RE) product manufacturing and applications can provide advanced technologies, exceptional professionals, knowledge, and management mechanisms from each participant. There should be encouragement for international cooperation prospects in RE policies for optimising social benefits.

Promoting research and development efforts and disseminating these technologies across borders is another effective method of energising cross-border energy trade. Adopting renewable energy technologies (RETs) across the four low and middle-income countries by building partnerships, relationships, and financing could help create an ecosystem of innovation. This approach could provide broader energy access to the rural population and ensure sustainability (Kruckenberg, 2015). Extension of the interconnected grids, as and where possible, and ensuring isolated grid and off-grid technologies, ideally based on renewable energy, for remote areas or dispersed populations, because it is often less costly than grid extension, would be a concrete way out to achieve universal energy access in the BBIN sub-region. Whereas the RETs, such as mini-grids that use hydro, wind, or hybrid systems and individual systems using solar PV or wind, are technically sound and cost-effective, their delivery mechanisms need to be well established and regulated.

By opening up the 'black box' of renewable energy partnerships, participants can gain deeper insights into the broader implications of RET programmes. Organising public research and development programmes to enable solutions for a tangible reduction of energy generation costs is critical. This would harness the talents, research instruments, knowledge, and other research resources across the countries. It could also help evaluate ways for cost-benefit analysis to implement the most sophisticated and relevant RE technologies appropriate for local conditions of economic and social development and resource availability. However, the caveat is that policies seeking short-term returns can cause a loss of social benefits at the national level since such intervention could bias investor decisions. The associated externalities produced due to their adoption, such as energy security and its correlation with education and healthcare services, would help improve the area's overall human capital. This fact should be widely publicised.

Certain policies can facilitate the transition to a low-carbon economy and promote green, resilient, and inclusive development (GRID) (Triyana and Li, 2022):

- Regulatory and fiscal interventions: In order to mobilise private sector investment, it is very important to address the political and regulatory uncertainties. Policies that align incentives to increase private sector involvement and reforms, such as repurposing current subsidies, would make renewable energy expansion financially attractive at a large scale in South Asian countries. For example, public-private partnerships (PPPs) can continue investing in energy-efficient technology to build the necessary infrastructure for the transition. An example of this is a PPP in India that is improving energy efficiency and enhancing business and public safety (Gupta, n.d.).
- Compensation of affected workers: Policymakers should consider the distributional impact of the energy transition by ensuring adequate compensation for those adversely affected. Specifically, in coal-dependent areas, non-renewable energy production firms and their workers are likely to be adversely affected by the green transition. Resources should be allocated to help affected firms diversify their production, create new jobs, and provide necessary job training to support low-skilled workers during the transition (Bluedorn and Hansen, 2022). Social protection programmes should be in place to safeguard workers and households adversely affected by the transition.
- Training for the future: Education and training should be focused on meeting future labour demands. For example, Nepal is applying the

GRID approach to build human capital, enhance built capital, and sustain natural capital (World Bank, 2022).

- Expansion of private sector participation: The scope for further private sector participation in hydropower development and associated power transmission should be expanded in Bhutan.
- Targeted assistance: Further targeted assistance, including detailed feasibility studies, financing mechanisms, and the formulation of public-private project implementation arrangements, should be provided to Nepal to strengthen its hydropower development framework.
- Harmonisation of the legal and regulatory frameworks for regional electricity trade: This would be a strong incentive for both public and private sector investment in cross-border power transmission facilities, as well as hydro and thermal power generating facilities, to provide additional power and exploit economies of scale for regional use (Rahman, 2012). The various investment agreements, trade agreements, and power purchase agreements involved could also benefit from the concerned countries being members of the Energy Charter Treaty (ECT). Such membership would provide greater security for cross-border energy transfer-related investments and agreements, as well as any dispute resolutions. The objective of the ECT is to strengthen the rule of law on energy issues by creating a level playing field of rules to be observed by all participating governments to minimise risks associated with energy-related regional investments and trade (Wijayatunga and Fernando, 2013).

Moreover, sub-regional groupings can also help achieve strategic goals for their members. Furthermore, a successful BBIN bloc may prove beneficial for the smaller states of Bangladesh, Bhutan, and Nepal, helping them fend off political manoeuvres by other countries, like China. Additionally, the challenges and processes involved in cross-border energy trade among the four countries may assist them in pursuing a larger and more integrated cooperative project.

The importance of political leadership cannot be underestimated. It plays a crucial role in addressing the specific challenges to energy cooperation that need to be addressed. This can be achieved through the following:

First, there is a need for the highest level of political leadership to champion energy cooperation. Second, leaders must portray energy cooperation as a means to provide access to the underprivileged and as a facilitator of poverty alleviation to gain acceptance for such projects among the wider population. Third, leaders should emphasise the benefits that can be derived from resource utilisation rather than engaging in political rhetoric about the total value of resource deposits in a particular constituency. India's leadership is indispensable for the realisation of energy projects. India must provide land access to Bangladesh for importing electricity from Nepal and Bhutan. Creating a regional hub in Siliguri, the small strip of Indian territory that separates Bangladesh, Nepal, and Bhutan, would have the necessary impact to stimulate a range of collaborative infrastructure and development projects, an opportunity that has been hindered by parochial perspectives on territorial control. Such articulation can potentially counter the widely held perception in South Asia that resources from a particular country should be used to ensure the energy security of the domestic population before being traded with a neighbouring state. Therefore, political perseverance in undertaking energy cooperation is recommended. With the support of political leadership, the realm of domestic consensus- building, positive engagement with extra-regional actors, effective articulation of the benefits of regional cooperation, and bridging gaps between key stakeholders become easier.

The government in New Delhi needs to gain the confidence of India's North-Eastern states. The Act East Policy, espoused by PM Modi, is a step in the right direction. In BBIN energy cooperation, India's

North-Eastern states have a greater role to play as several states are key stakeholders in the energy transmission projects. The immense natural resources there can be harnessed, and pragmatic energy projects can be undertaken. However, it is crucial to enhance the security architecture to prevent insurgent and terrorist groups from sabotaging the BBIN energy projects. In this scenario, successful hydroelectricity cooperation between BBIN countries can be pursued, including the implementation of adequate socio-economic programmes. Additionally, efforts should be made to moderate the propaganda spread by Nepali nationalist parties against India.

The availability of energy resources, potential for their economical exploitation, competitive cost advantages, adequate infrastructure, harmonious and enabling policies, lack of trade barriers, a climate of mutual trust, and strong political will to cooperate for gaining mutual benefits are prerequisites for cross-border energy trade. The dichotomy of exporting energy when shortfalls exist in the domestic market is arguably one of the biggest domestic political constraints to energy cooperation.

It is important to ensure that if the construction of a project results in any harm to the local population, they must be adequately compensated. It is important to ensure that local people are not exploited, as populations that live across the region's arbitrary and haphazard borders are some of the most vulnerable and destitute people in the world. For instance, in a hydro-energy project between India and Nepal, to address the disproportionate environmental cost borne by Nepal, a "beneficiary pay" principle can be implemented. Under this mechanism, the downstream country that benefits from upstream activities will compensate for the services rendered. To further ensure socio-economic safeguards, a group of independent experts should be employed to evaluate how the planning process of these projects can address local concerns of disenfranchisement, livelihoods, and exploitation. These initiatives can include infrastructure development, local employment generation, investment in education and healthcare, resettlement and rehabilitation, and a transparent benefit-sharing model.

Furthermore, it is important that politicians are open to listening to technocrats on how energy projects can have social, economic, and political impacts and whether these projects can empower people. The issue of empowerment is important as this is what politicians are interested in. If the research community can communicate to politicians that through energy cooperation, we can meet the aspirations of the people and empower them, then we can build political support for energy cooperation. Therefore, it is important that researchers and politicians learn to communicate and align their interests as a means of synchronising science and policy. Policymakers need to better understand the long-term value of partnerships, and detailed attention should be paid to organisational processes that facilitate inter-organisational learning (Romijn et al., 2010). The long-term value of partnerships not only includes the achievement of stated objectives but also results in greater trust and collaborations and may lead to long-term partnership agreements, joint initiatives, and continuous exchanges of knowledge and experience. While they can increase dependencies in the short term, they may allow for self-sufficiency in the long term if they involve the incremental transfer and translation of technological expertise and appropriate organisational capacities.

Furthermore, the sustainable transfer of renewable energy technologies might not be best achieved through the implementation of short-term renewable energy projects. Individual project partnerships may bridge specific resource, learning, implementation, and regulatory gaps, but due to their limited scope and duration, they are unlikely to permanently close them. The knowledge required to implement individual donor-initiated projects is fairly limited when compared to the knowledge needed to achieve a more sustainable uptake of renewable energy cooperation on a larger scale. The overall understanding of decarbonising BBIN is crucial since the sub-region has a high dependency on fossil fuel imports, and during times of geopolitical instability, such as the war in Ukraine, global energy prices skyrocket.

Policymakers must develop explicit learning objectives for their own organisations. Sustainable energy solutions are unlikely to be achieved by international experts who consider themselves solely as 'knowledge senders'. Failures in programme implementation are not merely a problem of implementing organisations but also a result of unsuitable policies and programme designs and of inter-organisational relationships failing to appropriately empower and incentivise renewable energy partnerships. If donor organisations consider the sustainable adoption of renewable energy and renewable energy technologies as their main objective, they should approach partnerships with local organisations as both a means and an end to achieve such outcomes.

Overcoming domestic political impediments to energy cooperation requires building consensus among political parties. Ruling parties in the region must undertake the difficult task of addressing any legitimate concerns that the opposition may have regarding energy trade with neighbouring states. In cases where political parties oppose projects simply to create deadlocks and impede progress, ruling parties must employ independent economists and environmental scientists to conduct studies on the impact of the energy projects. Ensuring access to information, freedom of the media, and an independent Environmental Impact Assessment can also build domestic consensus for energy projects. Broader dissemination of unbiased benefits through print and electronic media in South Asian countries should be encouraged.

To prevent corrupt practices by multinational corporations (MNCs), countries should consider implementing the Extractive Industries Transparency Initiative (EITI) Standards, a global standard that promotes accountability in the management of natural resources. Implementing the EITI standards would ensure that multilateral projects in South Asia are transparent, legal, and sustainable. The countries should also create an Energy Charter, similar to the International Energy Charter, which would reassure citizens of developing countries that their resources will not be siphoned off by corrupt government officials or MNCs. Additionally, the Energy Charter would provide citizens with a platform to lodge complaints. Therefore, it is important for the BBIN countries to consider the use of internationally accepted standards and legislation to ensure transparency and accountability in energy projects.

A reliable database is required to conduct realistic generation and transmission planning studies in a meaningful manner. Such a database would typically include detailed information for the countries considered, including power demand projections, existing systems and operating details, potential power supply expansion options with their capital costs and financing mechanisms, in-country power transfer options, cross-border power transfer options, and integrated and non-integrated power system operating procedures.

In the case of India and Bhutan, the Empowered Joint Group between India and Bhutan served a crucial purpose in reinvigorating the relationship in 2010. It helped streamline processes and eliminate various procedural bottlenecks. The group can be revitalised with regular meetings to resolve differences that can negatively impact cooperation. It can also contribute to revitalising the relatively slow progress in hydropower cooperation. Project implementation modalities present one of the biggest challenges in the relationship between the two countries. Since both countries are willing to make the implementation process more transparent and accountable, a framework that reflects the expectations of both parties can be established. A more equitable role for Bhutan, particularly as financial arrangements change, will be beneficial for both countries in the long run (Khillare and Kaithwar, 2022).

Political impediments to cooperation can be deeply rooted and influential, but they are not inevitable or unchangeable (Fierke, 1998). Astute political leadership at the highest level that supports and encourages regional causes at the core of domestic politics is needed, along with research collaboration on detailed blueprints of energy projects.

Key solutions to these problems involve promoting cross-border energy investments and regional energy trade to fully leverage the energy resources available within the region and its neighbouring countries (Behuria, 2009). Therefore, it is essential to create significant opportunities for cooperation and trade in the energy sector, ultimately aiming to establish one of the world's largest integrated energy markets.

Establishing transition pathways for renewable energy requires policy support that is durable and credible. This should be supplemented by intermediate targets that are monitored and, if necessary, revised. Specific advances would include:

Improving the enforcement of renewable energy purchase obligations (RPOs)

- Creating favourable land acquisition policies
- Establishing priority-sector lending for renewables
- Increasing outreach to banks and establishing a Green Bank
- Promoting energy efficiency and providing access to renewable-based energy

Creating an enabling business environment and improving the business models would help scale up renewable energy technologies in India. Unstable policies, administrative delays, bureaucratic malpractice, and a lack of clear information hinder the growth of renewables in the country's energy mix.

Other solutions include developing policy frameworks that provide a level playing field for renewable energy and facilitate market formation, ensuring transparent bidding processes with rigorous selection criteria and broad stakeholder participation, combating corruption, mobilising investments, reducing financing costs and currency risks through risk mitigation instruments and dedicated funds and facilities for renewables, and incorporating the true costs of fossil fuels in energy pricing by considering externalities related to air pollution and carbon emissions. There is an urgent need to enhance the robustness and capacity of India's transmission and distribution grid for a transition to a sustainable energy future.

Alongside integrating renewable power, India needs a holistic approach to energy development that recognises the linkages between electricity, heating, and transport needs. These linkages include not only emphasising the utilisation of renewable power in end-uses but also improving the collection and utilisation of biofuel wastes. To achieve this, there is a need to invest in more flexible and dispatchable capacity, demand-response mechanisms, interconnectors, and storage. Additionally, harnessing the synergies between the transport and power sectors can be beneficial. Incentivising renewable energy project developers, such as providing first access to the power grid through priority dispatch schemes, would promote greater coordination in the system. Information and communication technology (ICT) can also be utilised to manage peak loads, particularly in cities, and facilitate the integration of renewable power. Furthermore, a national bioenergy mission focused on meeting industrial energy demand, including increasing the collection of agricultural, forest, and waste materials, is necessary.

Efficient knowledge management requires regular data collection from developers regarding project status, annual capacity additions, and job creation. Information platforms for lending institutions should be established to encourage partnerships with banks. The objectives should not be compromised, and air pollution emission standards should be raised to the level of Organisation for Economic Cooperation and Development (OECD) countries. Unleashing innovation in renewable energy deployment requires a combination of technological improvements, new applications of existing technologies, the creation of new business or financing models, and inclusive policy mechanisms. India, facing challenges in accessing energy, has witnessed significant innovation in low-cost renewable applications and continually evolves distribution and financing models. Additional measures to foster innovative solutions include incorporating renewable energy standards into building codes for new urban buildings and promoting technological development in energy storage, energy monitoring, and system balance mechanisms (IRENA, 2017).

Among the BBIN countries, only Bangladesh lacks self-sufficiency in primary energy resources as compared to Nepal and Bhutan. Therefore, power trading among the four countries in this sub-region could be beneficial for all parties, with Bangladesh as a power recipient or importer, and Nepal and Bhutan as suppliers, while India is likely to play a dual role (Haque et al., 2020).

Delays in negotiating the necessary energy transit agreements have, at times, hindered the establishment of cross-border energy transfer infrastructure. However, investments in cross-border energy transfer infrastructure are now increasing, with efforts underway to expand supporting energy supply, develop realistic expectations of energy costs, deploy improved analytical techniques to assess interconnection viability, and implement more coherent legal and regulatory frameworks. The lag in cross-border energy trade investment in BBIN countries can be attributed to inadequate export-oriented energy development and unrealistic energy price expectations from prospective energy-receiving countries. Energy tariffs are often subsidised and kept below economic costs. Overcoming these challenges requires consistent efforts to engage with the obstacles, foster innovation, and promote new and renewable energy in the sub-region, leading to broad-based development cooperation that benefits the countries and their populations.

Regional cooperation is an excellent opportunity to promote sustainable growth by developing and sharing resources across the member countries rather than limiting their development within national boundaries. In BBIN's energy sector, this is particularly relevant due to the region's vast potential in underutilised renewable energy sources like hydropower, wind power, and solar power. Cooperation in this sector can enhance national energy security, reduce energy costs, and minimise the negative effects of energy price fluctuations. This will require various actions, such as building cross-border infrastructure and creating regional forums for sharing knowledge and experience (Rahman et al., 2012). The BBIN sub-region possesses vast untapped hydropower potential that can provide clean energy to even the remotest areas. Bhutan and Nepal, for instance, have significant hydro potential that is seasonal and dependent on water inflows, offering substantial opportunities for hydro generation capacities. Meanwhile, India and Bangladesh primarily rely on thermal-based power, and India has considerable wind and solar power potential. In addition to diverse energy resources, the sub-region exhibits complementary demand patterns that can be optimally harnessed to enhance energy access efficiently and reliably. Bangladesh experiences low electricity demand during winters, while Bhutan has lower demand during the monsoon season, exporting 70 per cent of its total power generation to India. In India, demand varies across regions, depending on the season.

With enormous energy mix and potential, yet underexploited to the benefit of the larger population of the BBIN sub-region, the lack of energy access is merely a small segment of the larger issue. Energy needs to be not only accessible and inclusive but also of high quality, reliable, and affordable. This means energy should be available whenever needed, in the necessary form, and at a price that the general population can afford. To provide modern energy services, there must be adequate infrastructure for production, transport, and distribution. This infrastructure should be constructed in the most cost-effective manner, balancing both short-term and long-term expenses while considering both positive and negative externalities. Additionally, it should aim to minimise the impact on climate change and be resilient to its effects. Since BBIN is one of the fastest developing and most vulnerable sub-regions to climate change, it should meet the increasing energy demand by investing in a low carbon economic development strategy (Gyanwali, 2020). Access to energy involves connecting unserved populations and maintaining or enhancing the quality, reliability, and affordability of energy services.

While this is true for all countries, in order to achieve the above in the BBIN sub-region, it becomes imperative for the member states to collaborate and share energy endowments so that the significant advantages would be able to percolate to the grassroots. A larger, more integrated energy system would reduce the need for reserves, would capitalise on the diversity of energy sources and consumption patterns, and would be better equipped to handle system fluctuations and variable generation. As discussed in the previous chapters, while unique characteristics of energy services exist in each country that may impede the functioning of efficient markets, it is essential to have institutions, regulations, policies, and mechanisms for information collection and dissemination. These elements guide participants in the energy sector, helping them understand the benefits, requirements, and limitations associated with their involvement, and ultimately enabling secure energy access by all stakeholders.

To sum up, since everyday life depends on access to modern forms of energy, therefore, access should be a basic right. Providing access to modern energy requires enormous investments in capital, infrastructure, and human resources, and energy cooperation in the BBIN region would ensure achievement of the objectives of quality, affordability, and environmental sustainability so that current and future generations will have a reliable energy supply. With relatively lesser degree of institutionalisation, the intensity of formal and informal engagements on regional cooperation in the sub-region has clearly increased compared to the broader regional grouping, the South Asian Association for Regional Cooperation (SAARC). Such collaboration can contribute significantly to achieving *Sustainable Energy for All* in the BBIN region, exemplifying Helen Keller's famous inspirational quote: "*Alone we can do so little; together we can do so much.*"

Bibliography

Abdullah-Al-Mahbub, M. and Abu Reza Md. Towfiqul Islam (2024), "Sustainable wind energy potential in Sandwip and Kalapara coastal regions of Bangladesh: A way of reducing carbon dioxide emissions", *Heliyon*, 10(1): e23982, https://doi.org/10.1016/j.heliyon.2024.e23982.

Acharya, A. (2004), "How ideas spread: whose norms matter? Norm localization and institutional change in Asian regionalism", *International Organization*, 58(2): 23975.

Acharya, Amitav (2007), "The Emerging Regional Architecture of World Politics", *World Politics* 59(4), pp. 629-652.

Adhikari, D. (2021), "Hydropower Development in Nepal", *Economic Review* Article, Nepal Rastra Bank, https://www.nrb.org.np/contents/uploads/2021/09/vol18_art4.pdf

Ahmed, S. and S.E. Ghani (2008), "Making Regional Cooperation Work for South Asia's Poor", *Economic Growth*.

Alam, F., Q. Alam, S. Reza, S. M. Khurshid-Ul-Alam, K. Saleque, and H. Chowdhury (2017a), "A Review of Hydropower Projects in Nepal", *Energy Procedia* 110, pp. 581–585.

Alam, F., Q. Alam, S. Reza, S. M. Khurshid-Ul-Alam, K. Saleque, and H. Chowdhury (2017b), "Sourcing Green Power in Bhutan: A Review", *Energy Procedia* 110, pp. 586–591.

Alam, F., R. Sarkar and Q. Alam (2019), "Power Generation and Regional Collaboration in South Asia", *Journal of the Institute of Engineering*, 15(3), pp. 28-32.

Ali, Muhammad (2014), "A Critical Study of Regionalism in South Asia", *The Dialogue*, 9(3), pp. 239-254.

Almulhem, Y. (2023), "Bhutan: The Role of Hydropower in Transforming the Economy", OPEC Fund Pavilion, 6 December 2023, https://opecfund.org/news/bhutan-the-role-of-hydropower-in-transforming-the-economy

Amin, A., Tooraj Jamasb, Manuel Llorca, Laura Marsiliani, and Thomas I. Renström (2022), "Decarbonisation policies and energy price reforms in Bangladesh", *Energy Policy*, 170(113224), pp. 1-10, https://doi.org/10.1016/j.enpol.2022.113224.

Ashman, D. (2001), "Strengthening North-South Partnerships for Sustainable Development", *Nonprofit and Voluntary Sector Quarterly*, 30, pp. 74–98, http://documents.worldbank.org/curated/en/099312405272210424/IDU0274da53607b1704a6c0beba048461972fe3e.

Ashraf, A.S.M.A. and M.S. Islam (2018), "Explaining Public Policy Choices: A Case Study of the First Nuclear Power Plant in Bangladesh", *Strategic Analysis* 42, pp. 503–523.

Asian Development Bank, 2005, "Technical Assistance South Asia Subregional Economic Cooperation III", Project Number: 37648, https://www.adb.org/sites/default/files/project-documents//37648-reg-tar.pdf

Asian Development Bank, 2010, "Bhutan: Energy Sector", Evaluation Study, Reference Number: SAP BHU 2010-21 Sector Assistance Program Evaluation, https://www.oecd.org/countries/bhutan/47177609.pdf.

Asian Development Bank, 2012, "Greater Mekong Subregion power trade and interconnection: 2 decades of cooperation", Manila: Asian Development Bank, https://www.adb.org/sites/default/files/publication/29982/gms-power-trade-interconnection.pdf

Asian Development Bank. 2013. South Asia Subregional Economic Cooperation, Manila, https://www.sasec.asia/uploads/publications/SASEC per cent20Expanded per cent20Brochure_2014_2.pdf

Asian Development Bank, 2015, "ADB to Help Scale Up India-Bangladesh Cross-Border Power Exchanges", October 1, 2015, https://www.adb.org/news/adb-help-scale-india-bangladesh-cross-border-power-exchanges.

Bäckstrand, K. (2008), :Accountability of Networked Climate Governance: The Rise of Transnational Climate Partnerships", *Global Environmental Politics*, 8(3), pp. 74–102.

Banerjee, S. and H. P. Gupta (2017), "The Evolution of the Indian Nuclear Power Programme", *Progress in Nuclear Energy* 101, pp. 4–18.

Basu, K. (2018), *The Republic of Beliefs: A New Approach to Law and Economics.* Princeton, NJ: Princeton University Press.

Barbieri, K. (1996), "Economic interdependence: A path to peace or a source of interstate conflict?" *Journal of Peace Research*, 33(1), pp. 29–49.

Barua, A. (2018), "Water diplomacy as an approach to regional cooperation in South Asia: a case from the Brahmaputra basin", *Journal of Hydrology*, 567, pp. 60–70.

Barua, A. and S. Vij (2018), "Treaties can be a non-starter: a multi-track and multilateral dialogue approach for Brahmaputra Basin", *Water Policy*, 20(5), pp. 1027–1041.

Batra, P. (2020), "Cross-border electricity trade brought to the forefront in the amendment to the Electricity Act 2003", *Infraline Plus*, 9(6), pp. 14-17.

Bazaz, A. B. and V. Seksaria (2014), "(De)Constructing India's and China's Energy and Climate Change Policy Choices: Interfaces of Co-operation", *Procedia- Social and Behavioural Sciences*, 157, pp. 322-329.

Behuria, Ashok (2009), *South Asia: The Quest for Regional Cooperation.* Institute for Defence Studies and Analyses (IDSA), New Delhi, pp. 69–70.

Bhatt, R.P. (2017), "Hydropower development in Nepal – Climate change, impacts and implications", *Renewable Hydropower Technologies*. Available at: https://doi.org/10.5772/66253.

Bhattacharjee, T., R. A. Deshpande and A. Chakraborty (2019), "Energy Integration in South Asia: A Status Review", *2019 IEEE International Conference on Sustainable Energy Technologies and Systems (ICSETS)*, Bhubaneswar, India, 2019, pp. 184-187.

Bhowmik, Shilajit Kar (2018), "Northeast India welcomes govt's decision to open Chittagong port", *Dhaka Tribune,* September 24, 2018, Available at: https://www.dhakatribune.com/bangladesh/government-affairs/2018/09/24/northeast-india-welcomes-govt-s-decision-to-open-chittagong-port.

Bisht, Medha (2011), "India-Bhutan Power Cooperation: Between Policy Overtures and Local Debates", *IDSA Issue Brief*, https://idsa.in/system/files/IB_IndiaBhutanPowerCooperation.pdf.

Bisht, Medha (2019), "From the edges of borders: reflections on water diplomacy in South Asia", *Water Policy,* 21(6), pp. 1123–1138.

Björn, Hettne and Fredrik Söderbaum (2000), "Theorising the Rise of Regionness", *New Political Economy,* 5, pp. 457-474.

Bluedorn, J. and Niels-Jakob Hansen (2022), *The Right Labor Market Policies Can Ease the Green Jobs Transition*, International Monetary Fund, April 13, 2022. Available at https://www.imf.org/en/Blogs/Articles/2022/04/13/blog041322-sm2022-weo-ch3.

Borzel, T. A. and T. Risse (2016), *The Oxford Handbook of Comparative Regionalism*. Oxford: Oxford University Press.

Bose, P.R. (2023), "All Powers Combined: Why It's Time For An India-Bangladesh-Bhutan-Nepal Regional Electricity Grid", *Swarajya Magazine*, January 9, 2023, https://swarajyamag.com/infrastructure/all-powers-combined-why-its-time-for-an-india-bangladesh-bhutan-nepal-regional-electricity-grid.

Brown, M. A., S. Zhou, and M. Ahmadi (2018), "Smart grid governance: An international review of evolving policy issues and innovations", *Wiley Interdisciplinary Reviews: Energy and Environment*, 7 (5), pp. 1–26.

Bremner, I. and A. Bailes (1998), "Sub-regionalism in the Newly Independent States", *International Affairs*, 74(1), pp. 131–147.

Business Insider Bureau, 2023, "Top 10 largest economies in the world", *Business Insider India*, April 17, 2023, https://www.businessinsider.in/top-10-largest-economies-in-the-world/articleshow/70547252.cms.

Buzan, Barry and Ole Weaver (2003), *Regions and Powers: The Structure of International Security*. Cambridge: Cambridge University Press.

Caniëls, M.C. and H.A. Romijn (2008), "Actor networks in strategic niche management: insights from social network theory", *Futures*, 40(7), pp. 613–629.

Central Electricity Authority, (2021), "Note on Cooperation with Bhutan", https://cea.nic.in/wp-content/uploads/hpi/2021/01/bhutan-12.pdf.

Chattopodhyay, Anirban (1997), "Some aspects of developmental regionalism", a Paper presented at 'Interactions with Indian Bordering States', Bangladesh Institute of International and Strategic Studies (BISS) Dhaka, February 19-20, 1997.

Chaturvedi, P., Z. Hussain and B. Nag (2015), "SAARC Geopolitics and Trade", *South Asian Survey, 22*, pp. 106-78.

Chaudhury, A.B.R., P. Basu and M. Bhonsale (2015), "Driving across the South Asian Borders: The motor vehicle agreement between Bhutan, Bangladesh, India and Nepal", Observer Research Foundation. Retrieved from https://www.orfonline.org/research/driving-acrossthe-south-asian-borders-the-motor-vehicle-agreement-between-bhutan-bangladesh-indiaand-nepal/.

Checkel, Jeffrey T. (1998), "The Constructivist Turn in International Relations Theory", *World Politics*, 50(2), pp. 324–48. Available at http://www.jstor.org/stable/25054040.

Chen, G. (2022), "An integrated electricity market in South Asia is key to energy security", *World Bank Blogs*, https://blogs.worldbank.org/endpovertyinsouthasia/integrated-electricity-market-south-asia-key-energy-security.

Confederation of Indian Industries (2023), "South Asia (BBIN) Power Summit 2023". Available at:https://powerexindia.in/media/downloads/Report_South%20Asia%20(BBIN)%20Power%20Summit%202023.pdf

Constitution of Nepal (2015), https://ag.gov.np/files/Constitution-of-Nepal_2072_Eng_www.moljpa.gov_.npDate-72_11_16.pdf, Accessed on June 2, 2023.

Cottey, A. (2009), "Sub-regional Cooperation in Europe: An Assessment", Bruges Regional Integration & Global Governance Papers 3/2009, https://cris.unu.edu/sites/cris.unu.edu/files/BRIGG_3-2009__revised_version.pdf.

Cutler, R.M. (2007), "Recent Developments in Cooperative Energy Security", *Oil, Gas & Energy Law Intelligence*, 5(4), pp. 1-19.

Das, D.K. (2002), *SAARC: Regional Cooperation and Development*. New Delhi, DEEP and Deep Publications.

Dash, K. C. (2008), *Regionalism in South Asia: Negotiating Cooperation, Institutional Structures*. London and New York, Routledge.

De, P. (2011), "Why is trade at borders a costly affair in South Asia? An empirical investigation", *Contemporary South Asia, 19*, pp. 441–464.

De, P. (2023), "Strengthening Regional Integration in South Asia: A Strategy Paper on Regional Connectivity and Trade Facilitation". RIS-DP # 288, https://ris.org.in/sites/default/files/Publication/DP-288_PrabirDe.pdf.

Deccan Herald (2024), "Nepal, India and Bangladesh to sign tripartite power trading deal on July 28", July 18, 2024, https://www.deccanherald.com/india/nepal-india-and-bangladesh-to-sign-tripartite-power-trading-deal-on-july-28-3111205.

Delinić, T. (2011), "SAARC – 25 Years of Regional Integration in South Asia". KAS International Papers, https://www.kas.de/c/document_library/get_file?groupId=252038&uuid=8a368f41-f5d0-6ffe-1d25-9a4a1a0a35a3.

Department of Electricity Development (2021), Ministry of Energy, Water Resource and irrigation, Government of Nepal. Available at: https://www.doed.gov.np/license/15

Department of Electricity Development, Government of Nepal (2024), "Power Plants: Hydro (More than 1MW)", http://www.doed.gov.np/license/54

Department of Food and Public Distribution, Government of India, n.d., "SAARC Food Bank", https://dfpd.gov.in/saarc-food-bank.htm.

Dhakal, S., P. Karki, and S. Shrestha (2019), "Cross-border electricity trade for Nepal: a SWOT-AHP analysis of barriers and opportunities based on stakeholders' perception", *International Journal of Water Resources Development*, 37:3, pp. 559-580, https://www.tandfonline.com/doi/abs/10.1080/07900627.2019.1648240?journalCode=cijw20

Dhungel, N. and S. Bhandari (2022), "Renewable energy and Nepal", *The Kathmandu Post*. 30 October, 2022, https://kathmandupost.com/columns/2022/10/30/renewable-energy-and-nepal.

Dixit, Kanak Mani (2014), "Semantics to Commerce: The Making of South Asia", *Asian Affairs*, 45(1), pp. 55-64, https://doi.org/10.1080/03068374.2013.876343.

Dorji, R. (2021), "Pandemic enhances cross-border electricity trade", *Kuensel*, July 30, 2022, https://kuenselonline.com/pandemic-enhances-cross-border-electricity-trade/.

Dorji, Yeshey (2016), *Water: Securing Bhutan's Future*, Asian Development Bank/National Environment Commission, Royal Government of Bhutan, Thimphu, Bhutan.

Dunne, Timothy, Milja Kurki and Steve Smith (2016), *International Relations Theories: Discipline and Diversity*. Oxford: Oxford University Press.

Elbers, W., L. Knippenberg, and L. Schulpen (2014), "Trust or control? Private development cooperation at the crossroads", *Public Administration and Development*, 34(1), pp. 1–13.

Ellersiek, A. (2011), *Same same but different. Power in partnerships. An Analysis of Origins, effects and Governance.* Doctoral Thesis, Tilburg.

Embassy of India, Thimphu (2016), The Third Joint Working Group (JWG) Meetings on Sub-Regional Cooperation between Bangladesh, Bhutan, India and Nepal (BBIN), Joint Press Release, (Dhaka, January 19-20, 2016), https://indembthimphu.gov.in/event.php?id=120.

Enerdata (2021), Bangladesh Energy Information, https://www.enerdata.net/estore/energy-market/bangladesh/.

Enerdata (2024), *World Energy & Climate Statistics – Yearbook 2024*, https://yearbook.enerdata.net/coal-lignite/coal-production-data.html

Export-Import Bank of India (2014), "Potential For Enhancing Intra-SAARC Trade: A Brief Analysis", Working paper No. 31, https://

www.eximbankindia.in/Assets/Dynamic/PDF/Publication-Resources/ResearchPapers/43file.pdf

Farnum R. L. (2018), "Drops of diplomacy: questioning the scale of hydro-diplomacy through fog-harvesting", *Journal of Hydrology,* 562, pp. 446–454.

Fawn, Rick (2009), "Regions and Their Study: Where from, What for and Where to?" *Review of International Studies,* 35, pp. 5-35.

Feng, J. (2022), "Five Cross-cutting Barriers to Bioenergy Deployment and How to Address Them", International Renewable Energy Agency, September 28, 2022, https://www.irena.org/News/expertinsights/2022/Sep/Five-cross-cutting-barriers-to-bioenergy-deployment-and-how-to-address-them

Fierke, Karin (1998), Changing Games, Changing Strategies: Critical Investigations in Security. Manchester: Manchester University Press.

Flyvbjerg, B. (2014), "What You Should Know about Megaprojects and Why: An Overview", *Project Management Journal,* 45(2), pp. 6–19.

Forsyth, T. (2012), "Reducing the Cost of Technology Transfer through Community Partnerships", in Ockwell, D.G., Mallett, A. (eds.), *Low-carbon technology transfer. From rhetoric to reality.* London: Routledge, pp. 340–353.

Fowler, A. (2000), "Introduction Beyond Partnership: Getting Real about NGO Relationships in the Aid System", *IDS Bulletin,* 31, pp. 1–13.

Garg, A.; V. Tiwari; and S. Vishwanathan (2017), *IOP Conference Series: Earth and Environmental Science.* 76:012001, https://iopscience.iop.org/article/10.1088/1755-1315/76/1/012001/pdf

Gartzke, E., and Q. Li (2003), "War, peace, and the invisible hand: Positive political externalities of economic globalization", *International Studies Quarterly,* 47(4), pp. 561–586.

Gippner, Olivia (2010), "Energy Cooperation in South Asia: Prospects and Challenges", South Asia Watch on Trade, Economics and Environment (SAWTEE), Kathmandu, Nepal.

Global Wind Atlas (2020), Available at: https://globalwindatlas.info/en/area/Nepal?print=true

Goel, S.N. (2023), "Integrating Power Markets: Enabling energy security for a sustainable South Asia", *Powerline,* March 10, 2023. Available at: https://powerline.net.in/2023/03/10/integrating-power-markets-enabling-energy-security-for-a-sustainable-south-asia/.

Gopalakrishnan, M. (2015), "Hydro Energy Sector in India: The Past, Present and Future Challenges", *Proceedings of the National Academy of Sciences,* 81, pp. 953–967.

Government of India (2020), Saubhagya Dashboard. Accessed June 23, 2024. Available at: https://saubhagya.gov.in/.

Government of India (2022), "India's Updated First Nationally Determined Contribution Under Paris Agreement (2021-2030)", https://unfccc.int/sites/default/files/NDC/2022-08/India%20Updated%20First%20Nationally%20Determined%20Contrib.pdf.

Government of Nepal (2020), "Second Nationally Determined Contribution (NDC)". December 8, 2020, https://climate.mohp.gov.np/attachments/article/167/Second%20Nationally%20Determined%20Contribution%20(NDC)%20-%202020.pdf.

Granado, Arze del J., D. Coady, and R. Gillingham (2010), "The Unequal Benefits of Fuel Subsidies: A Review of Evidence for Developing Countries", Working Paper WP/10/202. Washington, DC: Fiscal Affairs Department. International Monetary Fund.

Güney, T. (2019), "Renewable energy, non-renewable energy and sustainable development", *International Journal of Sustainable Development & World Ecology,* 26(5), pp. 389–397, https://doi.org/10.1080/13504509.2019.1595214.

Gupta, N. n.d. "Street Lighting PPPs: Improving Energy Efficiency and Public Safety in India's Cities". International Finance Commission, https://www.ifc.org/wps/wcm/connect/7db70379-e0fb-43e9-a89d-1ee97de2450e/PPP-Insights-India-PSL.pdf? MOD=AJPERES&CVID=nMdFg3.

Gyanwali, K.; R. Komiyama; Y. Fujii and T.R. Bajracharya (2020), "A review of energy sector in the BBIN sub-region", *International Journal of Sustainable Energy, 40*, pp. 530 - 556.

Gyeltshen, N. (2022), "Bhutan ramps up its solar ambitions", *The Dialogue Earth*, June 14, 2022, https://dialogue.earth/en/energy/bhutan-ramps-up-solar-energy-ambitions/

Haacke, J. (2003), *ASEAN'S Diplomatic and Security Culture: Development and Prospects*, Abingdon: Routledge.

Haas, M. (1989), *The Pacific Way: Regional Cooperation in the South Pacific*. New York: Praeger. p.16.

Hanasz, P. (2017), "Muddy waters: international actors and transboundary water cooperation in the Ganges-Brahmaputra problems", *Water Alternatives* 10 (2), pp. 459–474.

Haque, H.M. Enamul, Shobhakar Dhakal and S.M.G. Mostafa (2020), "An assessment of opportunities and challenges for cross-border electricity trade for Bangladesh using SWOT-AHP approach", *Energy Policy*, 137(111118), https://doi.org/10.1016/j.enpol.2019.111118.

Haran, V. P. (2018a), "Regional Cooperation in South Asia", *Indian Foreign Affairs Journal*, 13, pp. 195–208, https://www.questia.com/library/journal/1P4-2183491201/regionalcooperation-in-south-asia

Haran, V.P. (2018), "Water and hydropower cooperation in BBIN countries: Policies and way forward", *International Journal of Water Resources Development* 37(3), pp. 1–15, https://doi.org/10.1080/07900627.2018.1503076.

Haran, V.P. (2022), "Future of Hydropower Cooperation with Bhutan", Vivekananda International Foundation, May 11, 2022, https://www.vifindia.org/2022/may/11/future-of-hydropower-cooperation-with-bhutan.

Hasan, M., P. Dey, S. Janefar, N.A. Salsabil, I.J. Khan, N. Chowdhury, A. Arefin, and O. Farrok (2024), "A critical analysis of wind energy generation potential in different regions of Bangladesh", *Energy Reports*.

Hasan, M.Y., M. Monir, M.T. Ahmed, A.A. Aziz, S.M. Shovon, F.A. Akash, M.F.H. Khan, M.J. Faruque, M.S.I. Rifat, M.J. Hossain, P. Kundu, R. Akter and S.M. Ali (2021), "Sustainable energy sources in Bangladesh: A review on present and future prospect", *Renewable and Sustainable Energy Reviews*.

Hassan, M. (2016), "Prospect and so far, development of BBIN Connectivity", *International Journal of Social, Political, and Economic Research*, 1(1), pp. 15-29, https://ijosper.uk/index.php/i/article/view/11.

Hazarika, Natasha, Anamika Barua, Sumit Vij, Arundhati Deka and Lena Salame (2023), "Collective deliberation or just the state (in)action: How do we change the hydrodiplomacy landscape in South Asia?", *Water Policy*, 25 (1), pp. 15–22, https://doi.org/10.2166/wp.2023.166.

Health Effects Institute (2018), "State of Global Air 2018". Special Report. Boston, Massachusetts: Health Effects Institute, https://www.stateofglobalair.org/sites/default/files/soga-2018-report.pdf.

Hil Baky, M. A., M. M. Rahman, and A. K. M. S. Islam (2017), "Development of Renewable Energy Sector in Bangladesh: Current Status and Future Potentials", *Renewable & Sustainable Energy Reviews*, 73, pp. 1184–1197.

Hook, Glenn, and Ian Kearns (eds.) (1999), "Subregionalism and World Order". Basingstoke: Macmillan.

Hormats, Robert D. (1995), "Making Regionalism Safe", *Foreign Affairs*, p. 98.

Hossain, Ishtiaq (1997), "A Milestone Treaty between Dhaka and Delhi", *Trends* (Institute of Southeast Asian Studies, Singapore, with *Business Times,* April 7, 1997), p. 4.

Hossain, Ishtiaq (1998), "Bangladesh-India Relations: The Ganges Water-Sharing Treaty and Beyond", *Asian Affairs: An American Review* 25(3), pp. 131-150, https://www.jstor.org/stable/30172438.

Hossain, M. F., S. Hossain, and M. J. Uddin (2017), "Renewable Energy: Prospects and Trends in Bangladesh", *Renewable & Sustainable Energy Reviews* 70, pp. 44–49.

Huda, M.S. and S., Faiz (2011), "Bangladesh's Counterterrorism Successes", *Asian Conflicts Report,* Council for Asian Terrorism Research 20.

Huda, S.M., and M. McDonald (2016), "Regional cooperation on energy in South Asia: Unraveling the political challenges in implementing transnational pipelines and electricity Grids", *Energy Policy,* 98(C), pp. 73-83.

Huda, S.M. (2022), "Governance Challenges of South Asia's Energy Megaprojects", *Geopolitics,* 28(5), pp. 2142–2168, https://doi.org/10.1080/14650045.2022.2129011

Hurrell, A. (1995), "Explaining the Resurgence of Regionalism in World Politics", *Review of International Studies,* 21(4), pp. 331- 358, https://www.jstor.org/stable/20097421.

Hussain, A., G. K. Sarangi, A. Pandit, S. Ishaq, N. Mamnun, B. Ahmad and M. K. Jamil (2019), "Hydropower Development in the Hindu Kush Himalayan Region: Issues, Policies and Opportunities", *Renewable & Sustainable Energy Reviews* 107, pp. 446–461.

IEA (2023), "Nepal- Key energy statistics", 2020, https://www.iea.org/countries/nepal.

IHA (2019), *Hydropower sector climate resilience guide,* www.hydropower.org.

Indian Energy Exchange (IEX), 2021, "IEX Pioneers Cross Border Electricity Trade In An Endeavor Towards Building An Integrated South Asian Regional Power Market", April 19, 2021, https://www.iexindia.com/Uploads/PressRelease/19_04_2021Press%20Release%20-%20CBET%20Launch-19.4.21.pdf.

Infrastructure Development Company Limited (IDCOL), 2007, "Renewable Energy Projects", http://www.idcol.org/old/energyProject.php

International Energy Agency (IEA), 2020, "Bangladesh- Key energy statistics", https://www.iea.org/countries/bangladesh.

International Energy Agency (IEA), 2021, "India Energy Outlook 2021", https://iea.blob.core.windows.net/assets/1de6d91e-e23f-4e02-b1fb-51fdd6283b22/India_Energy_Outlook_2021.pdf.

International Energy Agency (IEA), 2023, "History: From oil security to steering the world toward secure and sustainable energy transitions", https://www.iea.org/about/history.

International Finance Commission (IFC). n.d., "Harnessing Nepal's Hydropower for Energy Starved South Asia", https://www.ifc.org/wps/wcm/connect/news_ext_content/ifc_external_corporate_site/news+and+events/news/nepal+hydropower.

International Monetary Fund (2022), "Climate Change: Fossil Fuel Subsidies". Washington, DC: IMF.

International Renewable Energy Agency (2022a), "Energy Profile- Bangladesh", https://www.irena.org/-/media/Files/IRENA/Agency/Statistics/Statistical_Profiles/Asia/Bangladesh_Asia_RE_SP.pdf.

International Renewable Energy Agency (2022b), "Energy Profile- Bhutan", https://www.irena.org/-/media/Files/IRENA/Agency/Statistics/Statistical_Profiles/Asia/Bhutan_Asia_RE_SP.pdf.

International Renewable Energy Agency (2022c), "Energy Profile- India", https://www.irena.org/-/media/Files/IRENA/Agency/Statistics/Statistical_Profiles/Asia/India_Asia_RE_SP.pdf.

International Renewable Energy Agency (2022d), "Energy Profile- Nepal", https://www.irena.org/-/media/Files/IRENA/Agency/Statistics/Statistical_Profiles/Asia/Nepal_Asia_RE_SP.pdf.

International Solar Alliance (2024), "About ISA", https://isolaralliance.org/about/background

Invest India (2024), "Industry Scenario", Updated on June 20, 2024, https://www.investindia.gov.in/sector/renewable-energy#:~:text=Renewable%20energy%20sources%20have%20a,Large%20Hydro:%2046.92%20GW

IRENA (2017), "Renewable Energy Prospects for India, a working paper based on RE map". The International Renewable Energy Agency (IRENA), Abu Dhabi, www.irena.org/remap.

Jauhari, Alka (2013), "India-Pakistan relations: international implications", *Asian Soc. Sci.* 9 (1), pp. 42–51.

Jha, R. (2011), "Total Run-of-River Type Hydropower Potential of Nepal", *Hydro Nepal: Journal of Water, Energy and Environment,* 7, pp. 7–13.

Jigang, W. and P. Webb (2020), "Special Report 5: International Energy Cooperation and Governance", in Shell International B.V. and The Development Research Center (DRC) of the State Council of the People's Republic of China (eds.) *China's Energy Revolution in the Context of the Global Energy Transition. Advances in Oil and Gas Exploration & Production.* Cham: Springer.

Kafle, U., T. Anderson and S.P. Lohani (2023), "The Potential for Rooftop Photovoltaic Systems in Nepal", *Energies*, 16, p. 747, https://doi.org/10.3390/en16020747

Karim, R., M. E. Karim, F. Muhammad-Sukki, S. H. Abu-Bakar, N. A. Bani, A. B. Munir, A. I. Kabir, J. A. Ardila-Rey, and A. A. Mas'ud (2018), "Nuclear Energy Development in Bangladesh: A Study of Opportunities and Challenges", *Energies* 11, pp. 1–15.

Katzenstein, P.J. (2005), *A World of Regions: Asia and Europe in the American Imperium.* Ithaca, New York: Cornell University Press.

Khillare, T. and R. Kaithwar (2022), "Hydrodiplomacy in South Asia: Challenges and Possibilities. Case of India and Bhutan". Council 1 For Strategic And Defense Research, https://csdronline.org/upload/user/CSDR_HSS_Paper_II.pdf.

Khosla, I.P. (ed.) (2005), *Energy and Diplomacy.* New Delhi: Konark Publishers.

Kibria, M.G., U.K. Paul, A. Hasan, M.S. Mohtasim, B.K. Das and M.M. Mourshed (2024), "Current prospects and challenges for biomass energy conversion in Bangladesh: Attaining sustainable development goals", *Biomass and Bioenergy*, p. 183, https://www.sciencedirect.com/science/article/abs/pii/S0961953424000928?via%3Dihub

Kruckenberg, L. J. (2015), "Renewable energy partnerships in development cooperation: Towards a relational understanding of technical assistance", *Energy Policy*, pp. 11-20.

Kumar, A. and S. Prasad (2023), "A Critical Assessment of Sustainable Development in the Indian Coal Mining Sector: A Review", *Revista Minelor – Mining Revue* 29(2), pp. 1-9, https://intapi.sciendo.com/pdf/10.2478/minrv-2023-0009

Kumar, Rakesh (2020), "India & South Asia: Geopolitics, regional trade and economic growth spillovers", *The Journal of International Trade & Economic Development*, 29(1), pp. 69-88, DOI: 10.1080/09638199.2019.1636121.

Kumar, S.; Priyanka and Anita Rani (2023), "Trends in India's exports of petroleum & crude products: A comprehensive analysis", *International*

Journal of Foreign Trade and International Business 2023; 5(2), pp. 01-07, https://foreigntradejournal.com/article/view/88/5-1-12

Kumaraswamy, P.R. and S. Datta (2006), "Bangladeshi gas misses India's energy drive?", *Energy Policy*, 34(15), pp. 1971-1973.

Lama, Mahendra P. (2000), "SAARC: Shallow regionalism, political abstinence and economic advocacy", *BIISS Journal*, 21 (1), pp. 1–34.

Larner, W. and W. Walters (2002), "The Political Rationality of "New Regionalism": Toward a Genealogy of the Region", *Theory and Society*, 31(3), pp. 391-432, https://www.jstor.org/stable/658132.

Lawson, S. (2006), *Culture and Context in World Politics*, Houndmills: Palgrave Macmillan, p. 150.

Lawson, S. (2009), "Asia/Europe and the construction of regional governance", in N. Thomas (ed.) *Regional Governance in the Asia-Pacific*, London: Routledge. p. 30120.

Lawson, S. (2016), "Regionalism, sub-regionalism and the politics of identity in Oceania", *The Pacific Review*, 29(3), pp. 387-409.

Lean, H. H. and R. Smyth (2014), "Electricity Consumption, Output, and Trade in Bhutan", ADB South Asia Working Paper Series.

Lister, S. (2000), "Power in partnership? An analysis of an NGO's relationships with its partners", *Journal of International Development*, 12, pp. 227–239.

Livemint, 2021, "Cross border electricity trade through power exchange begins". April 19, 2021, https://www.livemint.com/industry/energy/cross-border-electricity-trade-through-power-exchange-begins-11618827281432.html.

Lohani, S.P. and A. Blakers (2021), "100% renewable energy with pumped-hydro-energy storage in Nepal", *Clean Energy*, 5(2), pp. 243-253, https://doi.org/10.1093/ce/zkab011.

Lohani, S.P., P. Gurung, B. Gautam, U. Kafle, D. Fulford and M. Jeuland (2023), "Current status, prospects, and implications of renewable energy for achieving sustainable development goals in Nepal", *Sustainable Development*, 31(1), pp. 572-585.

Malla, A. and Dhananjayan, P. (2023), "Alternative renewable energy in Bhutan: Key findings and policy recommendations". (Working Paper). ICIMOD, https://doi. org/10.53055/ICIMOD.1022

Manoli, P. (2012), *The Dynamics of Black Sea Subregionalism*. London and New York: Routledge.

Mansfield, E.D. and H.V. Milner (1997), *The Political Economy of Regionalism*. New York: Columbia University Press.

Mansfield, E. D. and B.M. Pollins (2001), "The study of interdependence and conflict: Recent advances, open questions, and directions for future research", *Journal of Conflict Resolution*, 45(6), pp. 834–859.

Marzia, K., M. F. Hasan, T. Miyazaki, B. B. Saha, and S. Koyama (2018), "Key Factors of Solar Energy Progress in Bangladesh Until 2017", *Evergreen* 5, pp. 78–85.

Mawdsley, E. (2015), "DFID, the private sector and the re-centring of an economic growth agenda in international development", *Global Society* 29(3), pp. 339–358, https://doi.org/10.1080/13600826.2015.1031092.

McDonald, Matt (2013), "Constructivism", in Paul Williams (ed.), *Security Studies: An Introduction*. Routledge: New York, London, pp. 63–76.

Menezes, Debbie, Taylor Warren Henshaw and Cecile Fruman, *From Source to Sea: South Asia Water Initiative Completion Report 2013 - 2021 (English)*. Washington, D.C.: World Bank Group.

Merme, V., R. Ahlers and J. Gupta (2014), "Private equity, public affair: Hydropower financing in the Mekong Basin", *Global Environ*mental *Change*, 24, pp. 20–29, https://doi.org/10.1016/j.gloenvcha.2013.11.007.

Michael, Arndt (2013), *India's Foreign Policy and Regional Multilateralism*, Hampshire: Palgrave Macmillan. p. 92.

Ministry of Coal, Government of India (2018), "Coal Distribution and Marketing". Kolkata, India.

Ministry of Coal, Government of India (2024), "Coal Reserves", https://coal.gov.in/en/major-statistics/coal-reserves

Ministry of Commerce, Government of India (2017), "India's Duty Free Tariff Preference (DFTP) Scheme for Least Developed Countries (LDCs)", Version of October 9, 2017, https://commerce.gov.in/wp-content/uploads/2020/02/MOC_636434269763910839_international_tpp_DFTP.pdf.

Ministry of Economic Affairs, Royal Government of Bhutan (2021), "Bhutan Sustainable Hydropower Development Policy 2021", https://www.moenr.gov.bt/wp-content/uploads/2017/07/Sustainable-Hydropower-Development-Policy-2021-1.pdf

Ministry of Environment, Forests and Climate Change, Government of Bangladesh (2021), "Nationally Determined Contributions (NDCs) 2021 Bangladesh (Updated)", August 26, 2021, https://unfccc.int/sites/default/files/NDC/2022-06/NDC_submission_20210826revised.pdf.

Ministry of External Affairs, Government of India (2014), Joint Press Statement on the Visit of the Prime Minister to Nepal, August 4, 2014, https://www.mea.gov.in/bilateral-documents.htm?dtl/23807/Joint+Press+Statement+on+the+Visit+of+the+Prime+Minister+to+Nepal

Ministry of External Affairs, Government of India (2015a), Joint Statement on the meeting of the Ministers of Transport of Bangladesh, Bhutan, India, and Nepal on the Motor Vehicles Agreement, June 15, 2015, https://www.mea.gov.in/bilateral-documents.htm?dtl/25365/Joint+Statement+on+the+meeting+of+the+Ministers+of+Transport+of+Bangladesh+Bhutan+India+and+Nepal+on+the+Motor+Vehicles+Agreement

Ministry of External Affairs, Government of India (2015b), Prime Minister's press statement during joint press briefing with Prime Minister of Bangladesh. June 6, 2015, Available at: http://mea.gov.in/Speeches Statements.htm?dtl/25340/Prime_Ministers_Press_Statement_during_Joint_Press_Briefing_with_Prime_ Minister_of_Bangladesh.

Ministry of External Affairs (2023), English translation of Press Statement by Prime Minister Shri Narendra Modi during the visit of Prime Minister of Nepal, June 1, 2023, https://www.mea.gov.in/Speeches-Statements.htm?dtl/36631/English_translation_of_Press_Statement_by_Prime_Minister_Shri_Narendra_Modi_during_the_visit_of_Prime_Minister_of_Nepal

Ministry of Finance , Government of Nepal (2021), Economic Survey, https://www.mof.gov.np/uploads/document/file/1633341980_Economic%20Survey%20(English)%202020-21.pdf

Ministry of New and Renewable Energy (2022a), "Central Sector Scheme Biogas Programme (Detailed Implementation Guidelines)", Government of India, https://biogas.mnre.gov.in/public/downloadables/MNRE%20Biogas%20Prog%202021%20to%202026%20%20dated%2002_11_2022.pdf

Ministry of New and Renewable Energy (2022b), Annual Report 2021-22, https://mnre.gov.in/img/documents/uploads/file_f-1671012052530.pdf.

Ministry of New and Renewable Energy (2024a), "Hydropower-Overview". Government of India, https://mnre.gov.in/small-hydro-overview/

Ministry of New and Renewable Energy (2024), "Bio Energy Overview", https://mnre.gov.in/bio-energy-overview/

Ministry of Petroleum and Natural Gas (2023), "About International Cooperation", https://mopng.gov.in/en/international-cooperation/about-international-cooperation.

Ministry of Power, Government of India (2018), "Guidelines for import/export (cross-border) of electricity-2018". New Delhi, https://powermin.nic.in/sites/default/files/uploads/Guidelines_for_ImportExport_Cross%20Border_of_Electricity_2018.pdf

Ministry of Power, Government of India (2021), "Interconnection with neighbouring countries". August 9, 2021, https://powermin.gov.in/en/content/interconnection-neighbouring-countries.

Ministry of Power, Government of India (2022), "Power Sector at a Glance-All India", https://powermin.gov.in/en/content/power-sector-glance-all-india.

Ministry of Power, Government of India (2024), "FAQs on Hydropower". Government of India, https://powermin.gov.in/en/content/faqs-hydropower

Ministry of Statistics and Programme Implementation, Government of India (2023), "Energy Statistics- India 2023". National Statistical Office, https://www.mospi.gov.in/sites/default/files/publication_reports/Energy_Statistics_2023/Energy%20Statistics%20India%202023_07022024.pdf.

Mittleman, J. (1996), "Rethinking the "New Regionalism" in the Context of Globalization", *Global Governance*, 2(2), pp. 189-213, https://www.jstor.org/stable/27800136.

Modi, Narendra (2014), Text of Prime Minister's speech at 2014 SAARC Summit in Nepal, Available at: https://www.narendramodi.in/text-of-prime-ministers-speech-at-2014-saarc-summit-in-nepal-6941

Modi, Narendra (2024), "Joint Vision Statement on India - Bhutan Energy Partnership", March 22, 2024, https://www.narendramodi.in/joint-vision-statement-on-india-bhutan-energy-partnership-580863

Mohan, A. (2016), "The Future of Nuclear Energy in India", *Observer Research Foundation* 98, pp. 1–34.

Murthy, P. (2008), "SAARC and BIMSTEC-Understanding their Experience in Regional Cooperation". CUTS International.

Muzaffar, M., Iqra Jathol and Zahid Yaseen (2017), "SAARC: An Evaluation of its Achievements, Failures, and Compulsion for Cooperation", *Global Political Review*, 2(1), pp. 36-45.

Nanau, G. (2011), "The Wantok system as a socio-economic and political network in Melanesia", *Omnes: The Journal of Multicultural Society* 2(1), pp. 31-35.

National Environment Commission (2015), "Kingdom of Bhutan Intended Nationally Determined Contribution", September 30, 2015.

Nayak, N. R. (2023), "Energy and Development: Assessing the Viability of Hydroelectricity Trade in the Himalayas", *Strategic Analysis* 43(3), pp. 215-234.

Nepal Energy Efficiency Programme (2024). Available at: http://energyefficiency.gov.np/article-energy_situation_nepal, Accessed on June 2, 2023.

Nepali, B. (2023), "Opportunities and Challenges in Bangladesh, Bhutan, India, and Nepal (BBIN) Initiative for Nepal", *Prashasan*, Ministry of Federal Affairs and General Administration, July 2023, Vol. 55, Issue 1, No. 137, pp. 71-85.

Newell, P., N. Jenner and L. Baker (2009), "Governing Clean Development: A Framework for Analysis", *Development Policy Review*, 27, pp. 717–739.

Ngampramuan, S. and C. Ploberger (2020), *Sub-regionalism and International River Basins: Evaluating the Integration of the Mekong and Danube*. UK, Cambridge Scholars Publishing, p. 16.

Niaz, Muhammad Tariq (2022), "Regional Integration in South Asia: Utopia or Reality?", *Margalla Papers* 26 (1), pp. 108-120.

NITI Aayog Government of India (2018), Draft National Energy Policy. New Delhi, India.

Nuruzzaman, M. (1999), "SAARC and subregional cooperation: Domestic politics and foreign policies in South Asia", *Contemporary South Asia*, 8(3), pp. 311-322, DOI: 10.1080/09584939908719871.

Nye, J. S. (ed.). (1968), *International Regionalism: Readings*. Boston: Little, Brown and Co.

O'Leary, D. T., J.P. Charpentier and D. Minogue (1998), "Promoting regional power trade- the Southern African Power Pool", p. 346. Washington, D.C.: The World Bank.

Pal, P. (2016), "Intra-BBIN Trade: Opportunities and Challenges", *Observer Research Foundation* 135, pp. 1–7.

Passi, A. (2009), "The resurgence of the "region" and "regional identity": Theoretical perspectives and empirical observations on regional dynamics in Europe", *Review of International Studies* 35(S1), pp. 121-146.

Phillips, N. (2001), "Regionalist Governance in the New Political Economy of Development: "Relaunching" the Mercosur", *Third World Quarterly*, 22(4), pp. 565–583, quoted in Kanishka Jayasuriya, "Governing the Asia

Pacific: Beyond the "New Regionalism"", *Third World Quarterly*, 24(2), 2003, pp. 199–215.

Pillai, A.V. and S. Prasai (2021), "The political economy of electricity trade and hydropower development in eastern South Asia", *International Journal of Water Resources Development* 37(3), pp. 411–423.

Pinkse, J., A. Kolk (2012), "Addressing the Climate Change - Sustainable Development Nexus: The Role of Multistakeholder Partnerships", *Business & Society*: 51, pp. 176–210.

Podder, A.K.; M. Habibullah; N. K. Roy and H. R. Pota (2021), "A chronological review of prospects of solar photovoltaic systems in Bangladesh: Feasibility study analysis, policies, barriers, and recommendations", *IET Renewable Power Generation*, 15, pp. 2109–2132, https://ietresearch.onlinelibrary.wiley.com/doi/epdf/10.1049/rpg2.12165

Pohl, B. and A. Swain (2017), "Leveraging diplomacy for resolving transboundary water problems", In Islam S. and K. Madani K. (eds.) *Water Diplomacy in Action: Contingent Approaches to Managing Complex Water Problems.* London: Anthem Press, pp. 19–34.

Pokharel, S. (2001), "Hydropower for Energy in Nepal", *Mountain Research and Development*, 21(1), pp. 4–9. Available at: https://doi.org/10.1659/0276-4741(2001)021[0004:HFEIN]2.0.CO;2.

Pondyal, K.N., B.K. Bhattarai, Sapkota B, and Kjeldstad, B. (2011), "Solar radiation potential at four sites of Nepal", *Journal of Institute of Engineering*, 8(3), pp. 189–197.

Porta, E. L. and A.T. Wolf (2021), "Intrinsic and spiritual dimensions of water at the local scale, and the disconnect with international institutions", *Sustainability*, 13(16), p. 8948.

Premkumar, Lakshmi (2016), "A study of the India-Bhutan Energy Cooperation Agreements and the Implementation of Hydropower Projects in Bhutan", Vasudha Foundation, 2016, http://www.vasudha-foundation.org/wp-content/uploads/Final-Bhutan-Report_30th-Mar-2016.pdf.

Press Information Bureau, Government of India, Ministry of Power (2011), "India to Develop 10,000MW Hydro Power in Bhutan". November 25, 2011, https://pib.gov.in/newsite/PrintRelease.aspx?relid=77616.

Press Information Bureau (2020), "PM's Remarks on Way Forward at Video Conference of SAARC. Leaders on combating COVID-19", Prime Minister's Office. March 15, 2020, https://pib.gov.in/PressReleasePage.aspx?PRID=1606468.

Press Information Bureau (2021), "National Action Plan on Climate Change (NAPCC)", Ministry of Environment, Forest and Climate Change, Government of India, https://static.pib.gov.in/WriteReadData/specificdocs/documents/2021/dec/doc202112101.pdf

Press Information Bureau (2023a), "Availability of Coal Reserves in The Country". Ministry of Coal, Government of India, https://pib.gov.in/PressReleasePage.aspx?PRID=1909977

Press Information Bureau (2023b), "Rajasthan, Gujarat and Tamil Nadu emerge Top Achievers in Wind Energy Adoption: India celebrates Global Wind Day; day-long celebration explores ways to Power the Future of India using Wind Energy", Ministry of New and Renewable Energy, Government of India, June 15, 2023, https://pib.gov.in/PressReleaseIframePage.aspx?PRID=1932715

Press Information Bureau (2023c), " Installed Wind Energy Capacity in the country is 43.7 GW, likely to increase to 99.9 GW by 2029-30: New & Renewable Energy Minister", Ministry of New and Renewable Energy, August 1, 2023, https://pib.gov.in/PressReleasePage.aspx?PRID=1944759

Press Information Bureau (2023d), "10,232 MW of installed capacity of Biomass Power, Bagasse Cogeneration and Non-bagasse Cogeneration Plant in India with Maharashtra and UP accounting for nearly 45% of installed capacity: Union Power & NRE Minister Shri R. K. Singh", Ministry of New and Renewable Energy, March 28, 2023, https://pib.gov.in/PressReleaseIframePage.aspx?PRID=1911482

Power Division, Ministry of Power, Energy, and Mineral Resources (2015), "Scaling Up Renewable Energy in Low Income Countries (SREP) Investment Plan for Bangladesh", Sustainable & Renewable Energy Development Authority, Government of the People's Republic of Bangladesh, https://www.cif.org/sites/cif_enc/files/bangladesh_srep_ip_final.pdf

Rai, N. P. Shrestha, and S. Neupane (2016), "Engaging in reforming policies in Nepal: an analytical documentation of the Niti Foundation's experience in Nepal's hydropower sector", DFAT-TAF Partnership Working Paper Series 5, The Asia Foundation, San Francisco, USA.

Rahaman, M.M. and M.S. Hossain (2020), "Hydropower development along the major rivers basins in South Asia: benefits for Bangladesh", *Sustainable Water Resources Management,* 6(116). https://doi.org/10.1007/s40899-020-00479-4.

Rahman, S., P. D.C. Wijayatunga, H. Gunatilake, and P. N. Fernando (2012), *Energy Trade in South Asia: Opportunities and Challenges*. Manila, Philippines: Asian Development Bank.

Ramani, K. (2004), "Energy for sustainable development: Challenges for Asia and the Pacific and lessons from UNDP projects in the region". New York, US: UNDP: 108.

Rana, A.P. (2003), "'New Directions' in the study of SAARC: Evaluating the bases of regional cooperation in South Asia", *South Asian Survey* 10 (1), pp. 13–29.

Rao, P. V. (2012), "South Asia's retarded regionalism", *Journal of the Indian Ocean Region*, 8(1), pp. 37–53.

Ravi, S. (2014), "Developing SAARC's Higher Education Potential", *Brookings India Briefing Book*, Brookings India Institute, November 20, 2014, https://www.brookings.edu/research/developing-saarcs-higher-education-potential/.

Ray, P. A., L. Bonzanigo, S. Wi, Y.C. E. Yang, P. Karki, L.E. Gracia, D.J. Rodriguez, and C.M. Brown (2018), "Multidimensional stress test for hydropower investments facing climate, geophysical and financial uncertainty", *Global Environmental Change*, 48, pp.168–181, https://doi.org/10.1016/j.gloenvcha.2017.11.013.

Rijal, P. (2019), "Nepal, Bangladesh to use Indian grid for power trade", *The Kathmandu Post*, June 23, 2019, https://kathmandupost.com/money/2019/06/23/nepal-bangladesh-to-use-indian-grid-for-power-trade.

Ríos-Mercado, R.Z. and C. Borraz-Sánchez (2015), "Optimization problems in natural gas transportation systems: A state-of-the-art review", *Applied Energy*, 147, pp. 536-555.

RMA. Annual Report 2020. Royal Monetary Authority of Bhutan, 2020.

Romijn, H., R. Raven, I. de Visser (2010), "Biomass energy experiments in rural India: insights from learning-based development approaches and lessons for Strategic Niche Management", *Environmental Science and Policy*, 13, pp. 326–338.

Roy, A.D. (2023), "Why the movement against Rampal plant in Bangladesh failed", *Himal Southasian*, February 24, 2023.

Russett, Bruce M. (1969), "International Regimes and the Study of Regions", *International Studies Quarterly*, 13:(4).

Rynning, Sten (2017), "South Asia and the great powers: International relations and regional Security". London: I.B. Tauris.

SAARC Charter. n.d, https://www.saarc-sec.org/index.php/resources/agreements-conventions/46-saarc-charter-provisional-rules-of-procedure/file.

SAARC Development Fund n.d. "Background of SDF", http://www.sdfsec.org/about-sdf.

SAARC (2004), "Agreement on South Asian Free Trade Area (SAFTA)", https://www.saarc-sec.org/index.php/resources/agreements-conventions/36-agreement-on-south-asian-free-trade-area-safta/file.

SAARC (2005), "Agreement for Establishment of SAARC Arbitration Council", https://www.saarc-sec.org/index.php/resources/agreements-conventions/28-agreement-for-establishment-of-saarc-arbitration-council/file.

SAARC (2007a), "Agreement on Establishing the SAARC Food Bank", https://www.saarc-sec.org/index.php/resources/agreements-conventions/31-agreement-on-establishing-the-saarc-food-bank/file.

SAARC (2007b), "Agreement for Establishment of South Asian University", https://www.saarc-sec.org/index.php/resources/agreements-conventions/29-agreement-for-establishment-of-south-asian-univeristy/file.

SAARC (2008a), "Charter of the SAARC Development Fund (SDF)", https://www.saarc-sec.org/index.php/resources/agreements-conventions/38-charter-of-the-saarc-development-fund/file.

SAARC (2008b), "Agreement on the Establishment of South Asian Regional Standards Organisation (SARSO)", https://www.saarc-sec.org/index.php/resources/agreements-conventions/37-agreement-on-the-establishment-of-south-asian-regional-standards-organisation/file.

Saklani, Udisha and Cecilia Tortajada (2019), "India's Development Cooperation in Bhutan's Hydropower Sector: Concerns and Public Perceptions", *Water Alternatives*, 12(2), pp. 734-759.

Saklani, Udisha, Padmendra P. Shrestha, Aditi Mukherji and Christopher A. Scott (2020), "Hydro-energy cooperation in South Asia: Prospects for transboundary energy and water security", *Environmental Science and Policy*, 114(5), pp. 22-34.

Sarker, T., S. Hossain, and K. M. N. Islam (2020), "Role of Regional Cooperation and Integration in Improving Energy Insecurity in South Asia". ADBI Working Paper 1120. Tokyo: Asian Development Bank Institute. Available: https://www.adb.org/publications/role-regionalcooperation-integration-improving-energy-insecurity-south-asia

SASEC, 2013, "Key facts-Energy", https://www.sasec.asia/index.php?page=energy.

SASEC, 2022, "Bhutan Sees Rise in Cross-border Electricity Trade in 2020", July 30, 2022, https://www.sasec.asia/index.php?page=news&nid=1412&url=bhu-cross-border-energy-trade-rises-pandemic.

Sawhney, A. & Kumar, R. (2008), "Rejuvenating SAARC: The Strategic Payoffs for India", *Global Economy Journal,* 8.

Schelling, T. (1960), "The strategy of conflict". Cambridge, MA: Harvard University Press.

Scheyvens, R., G. Banks and E. Hughes (2016), "The private sector and the SDGs: the need to move beyond 'business as usual'", *Sustain*able *Development*, 24 (6), pp. 371–382, https://onlinelibrary.wiley.com/doi/10.1002/sd.1623.

Sharif, S.I., M.A.R. Anik, M. Al-Amin, and M.A.B. Siddique (2018), "The Prospect of Renewable Energy Resources in Bangladesh: A Study to Achieve the National Power Demand", *Energy and Power* 8, pp. 1–6.

Sharma, D. (2021), "The Significance of Jaldhaka Hydro Power Project in Bhutan- India Partnership", *Kuensel,* August 28, 2021, https://kuenselonline.com/the-significance-of-jaldhaka-hydro-power-project-in-bhutan-india-partnership/.

Sharma, G. (2019), "India and Nepal open South Asia's first cross-border oil pipeline", *Reuters*, September 10, 2019, https://www.reuters.com/article/us-nepal-india-idUSKCN1VV135.

Sharma, S. (2017), "Trickle to torrent to irrelevance? Six decades of foreign aid in Nepal", in D. Gyawali, M. Thompson, M. Verweij (eds.), *Aid, technology and development: The Lessons from Nepal,* London: Routledge, pp. 54–74, https://doi.org/10.4324/9781315621630-14.

Shidore, S. and J. W. Busby (2019), "One More Try: The International Solar Alliance and India's Search for Geopolitical Influence", *Energy Strategy Reviews* 26, https://www.sciencedirect.com/science/article/pii/S2211467X19300781

Shrestha, R.S. (2009), Article on electricity import from India. July 7, 2009, http://www.ratnasansar.com/2009/07/

Shukla, Akash Kumar, K. Sudhakar, Prashant Baredar, (2017), "Renewable energy resources in South Asian countries: Challenges, policy and recommendations", *Resource-Efficient Technologies,* 3(3), pp. 342-346, https://www.sciencedirect.com/science/article/pii/S2405653716302299#:~:text=At%20the%20South%20Asia%20region,and%20enhance%20stable%20economic%20growth.

Shukla, Ashish (2019), "Sub-regional Cooperation under BBIN Framework: An Analysis", ICWA, https://www.icwa.in/show_content.php?lang=1&level=3&ls_id=4817&lid=2833.

Sikri, V. (2015), "The Modi factor", *The Daily Star*, June 6, 2015, https://www.thedailystar.net/op-ed/politics/the-modi-factor-92809.

Singh, B.K. (2013), "South Asia Energy Security: Challenges and Opportunities", *Energy Policy* 63, pp. 458–468.

Söderbaum, F. (2013), "Rethinking Regions and Regionalism", *Georgetown Journal of International Affairs,* 14(2), pp. 9-18.

Sondhi, Sunil (2006), "South Asia in international relations", *South Asia Politics,* 4(11).

Solar Electric Manufacturer's Association Nepal (SEMAN) (2019), "Solar Energy technology in Nepal", https://www.semannepal.org.np/publications/solar-energy-technology-in-nepal.

South Asia Regional Energy Partnership (2023), Study on International Best Practice for Developing Cross-Border Electricity Transmission Infrastructure, Draft Interim Report, USAID, https://sarepenergy.net/wp-content/uploads/2024/03/X-Border-Transmission-Development-Business-and-Financial-Models.pdf

Sovacool, B.K. (2012), "Design principles for renewable energy programs in developing countries", *Energy & Environmental Science,* 5, pp. 9157–9162.

Srivastava, L. and N. Misra, (2007), "Promoting Regional energy cooperation in South Asia", *Energy Policy* 35(6), pp. 3360-3368.

Statista (2022), "Leading countries in electricity generation worldwide in 2021", https://www.statista.com/statistics/1263669/electricity-generation-worldwide-country/.

Sustainable and Renewable Energy Development Authority (2015), "Scaling Up Renewable Energy in Low Income Countries (SREP) Investment Plan for Bangladesh". Dhaka, Bangladesh.

Szulecki, K., P. Pattberg, F.Biermann (2011), "Explaining Variation in the Effectiveness of Transnational Energy Partnerships", *Governance*, 24, pp. 713–736.

T. Pasanen, B. Befani, N. Rai, S. Neupane, H. Jones and D. Stein (2019), "What drives policy change in Nepal? A qualitative comparative analysis", Overseas Development Institute, London, UK.

Tang, M. and M. Thant (1994), "Growth Triangles: Conceptual Issues and Operational Problems". Staff Paper No. 54, Asian Development Bank, https://www.adb.org/sites/default/files/publication/28150/es54.pdf.

Thapa, K. (2022)", "Nuwakot solar power station begins supplying electricity to Kathmandu", *The Kathmandu Post*, September 15, 2022, https://kathmandupost.com/money/2022/09/14/nuwakot-solar-power-station-begins-supplying-electricity-to-kathmandu

The Economic Times (2024), "Hydroelectric surge: India on the cusp of a significant transformation in its energy sector", April 6, 2024, https://economictimes.indiatimes.com/industry/renewables/hydroelectric-surge-india-on-the-cusp-of-a-significant-transformation-in-its-energy-sector/articleshow/109082674.cms?from=mdr

The Hindu (2021), "India needs to tap hydro resources to achieve 500 GW renewable energy capacity target: Power Minister R. K. Singh". November 8, 2021, https://www.thehindu.com/business/Industry/india-needs-to-tap-hydro-resources-to-achieve-500gw-renewable-energy-capacity-target-power-minister-r-k-singh/article37377007.ece.

The Kathmandu Post (2023), "NEA decides to sign PPAs for 1500MW non-storage projects", February 10, 2023, https://kathmandupost.com/national/2023/02/10/nea-decides-to-sign-ppas-with-developers-of-1500mw-run-of-the-river-hydel-projects.

The Wire. 2024. "India, Nepal Ink Agreement on Export of 10,000 MW of Electricity", January 4, 2024, https://thewire.in/south-asia/india-nepal-ink-agreement-on-export-of-10000-mw-of-electricity

Third Joint Working Group (JWG) Meeting on Sub-Regional Cooperation between Bangladesh, Bhutan, India and Nepal (BBIN), http://mea.gov.in/press-releases.htm?dtl/26284/Third_Joint_Working_Group_JWG_Meetings_on_SubRegional_Cooperation_between_Bangladesh_Bhutan_India_and_Nepal_BBIN_January_1920_2016.

Tortajada, C. and U. Saklani (2018), "Hydropower-based collaboration in South Asia: The case of India and Bhutan", *Energy Policy* 117, pp. 316–325, https://doi.org/10.1016/j.enpol.2018.02.046.

Tripathi, L., A. K. Mishra, A. K. Dubey, C. B. Tripathi, and P. Baredar (2016), "Renewable Energy: An Overview on its Contribution in Current Energy Scenario of India", *Renewable & Sustainable Energy Reviews* 60, pp. 226–233.

Triyana, Y. and Li, Yi (Claire) (2022), "Green Energy Can Accelerate Sustainable Growth Across South Asia", *World Bank Blogs*, October 19, 2022, https://blogs.worldbank.org/endpovertyinsouthasia/green-energy-can-accelerate-sustainable-growth-across-south-asia.

Tshreing, S. and B. Tamang (n.d.) *Hydropower - Key to sustainable, socio-economic development of Bhutan.* United Nations, https://www.un.org/esa/sustdev/sdissues/energy/op/hydro_tsheringbhutan.pdf.

Uddin, M.N. (2022), "Gondwana Deposits of the Bengal Basin (Bangladesh) and Coal Potential" in Chowdhury et al., (eds.) *Bangladesh Geosciences and Resources Potential*, CRC Press: Boca Raton.

Us Salehin, M. (2024), "Overview of the Hydropower Perspective of Bangladesh". Available at: https://ssrn.com/abstract=4709543

United Nations, Sustainable Water and Energy Solutions Network (n.d.) International Cooperation, https://www.un.org/en/water-energy-network/page/international-cooperation.

United Nations (2013), "An investment guide to Bhutan Opportunities and Conditions 2013". UNCTAD/DIAE/ITI/2013/1, https://theiguides.org/guides/bhutan.pdf

United Nations Development Programme (2021), "Bhutan launches its first grid-tied solar power plant". October 4, 2021, https://www.undp.org/bhutan/press-releases/bhutan-launches-its-first-grid-tied-solar-power-plant

United States Agency for International Development (USAID) (2018), "Nepal Hydropower Development Program". Available at: https://www.usaid.gov/nepal/fact-sheets/nepal-hydropower-development-progr2am.

Uprety K. and S.M. Salman (2011), "Legal aspects of sharing and management of transboundary waters in South Asia: preventing conflicts and promoting cooperation", *Hydrological Sciences Journal*, 56(4), pp. 641–661.

Vaidya, Ramesh Ananda, David James Molden, Arun Bhakta Shrestha, Nisha Wagle and Cecilia Tortajada (2021a), "The role of hydropower in South Asia's energy future", *International Journal of Water Resources Development*, 37(3), pp. 367-391.

Vaidya, R.A., N. Yadav, N. Rai, S. Neupane and A. Mukherji (2021b), "Electricity trade and cooperation in the BBIN region: lessons from global experience", *International Journal of Water Resources Development* 37(3), pp. 439-465.

Van de Graaf, T. and J. Colgan (2016), "Global Energy Governance: A Review and Research Agenda", *Palgrave Commun*, 2(1).

Van Huijstee, M.M., M. Francken, M., P. Leroy (2007), "Partnerships for sustainable development: a review of current literature", *Environmental Sciences*, 4, pp. 75–89.

Vincent, R. and A. Byrne (2006), "Enhancing learning in development partnerships", *Development in Practice*, 16, pp. 385–399.

Viotti, Paul R. and Mark V. Kauppi (2012), *International Relations Theory*. Longman, Boston.

Warleigh-Lack, Alex (2006), "Towards a Conceptual Framework for Regionalisation: Bridging 'New Regionalism' and 'Integration Theory'", *Review of International Political Economy*, 13(5), pp. 750-771, https://www.jstor.org/stable/25124101.

Wendt, A. (1992), "Anarchy is what States Make of it: The Social Construction of Power Politics", *International Organisation*, 46(2), pp. 391-425.

Wendt, A. (1995), "Collective Identity Formation and the International State", *The American Political Science Review*, 88(2), pp. 384-396, https://doi.org/10.2307/2944711.

Wijayatunga, P. and P.N. Fernando (2013), *An Overview of Energy Cooperation in South Asia*. Asian Development Bank, http://hdl.handle.net/11540/2321.

Wolf, A. T. and Z. Shubber (2020), Webinar Series on Hydrodiplomacy [Webinar]. Indian Institute of Technology, Guwahati, https://www.youtube.com/channel/UCsSi2Cw12GErTYIT7CA2HSQ.

World Bank Data (2023), "Renewable energy consumption (% of total final energy consumption) - South Asia", https://data.worldbank.org/indicator/EG.FEC.RNEW.ZS?locations=8S.

World Bank Group (2022), Bangladesh Country Climate and Development Report. CCDR Series. World Bank Group, Washington, DC, https://openknowledge.worldbank.org/server/api/core/bitstreams/6d66e133-e49d-5ad9-b056-7b1a6c6206ed/content.

World Bank. (n.d.). "Why #OneSouthAsia?" Available at: https://www.worldbank.org/en/programs/south-asia-regional-integration/overview.

World Bank (2016), "The Potential of Intra-regional Trade for South Asia", https://www.worldbank.org/en/news/infographic/2016/05/24/the-potential-of-intra-regional-trade-for-south-asia, Accessed on 2 February 2022.

World Bank (2017), "World Bank Board Approves US$100 million for Large-Scale Solar Parks in India", March 30, 2017, https://www.worldbank.org/en/news/press-release/2017/03/30/world-bank-board-approves-usd100-million-large-scale-solar-parks-india.

World Bank (2021), "India's Solar Learning Curve Inspires Action Across the World". Feature Story, July 9, 2021, https://www.worldbank.org/en/news/feature/2021/07/09/india-s-solar-learning-curve-inspires-action-across-the-world.

World Bank (2021), "Why #OneSouthAsia? Our regional strategy to build a stronger South Asia", September 28, 2021, https://www.worldbank.org/content/dam/videos/sar/2021/sep/Rice%20Final.mp4.

World Bank (2022), "Green, Resilient, Inclusive Development (GRID) in Action: A High-level Dialogue for Nepal", June 21, 2022, https://www.worldbank.org/en/events/2022/06/13/green-resilient-inclusive-development-grid-in-action-a-high-level-dialogue-for-nepal.

World Bank (2007), "Bhutan Hydropower Sector Study: Opportunities and Strategic Options". Energy Sector Management Assistance Program (ESMAP) Paper. ESM 119/07. Washington, DC, https://openknowledge.worldbank.org/server/api/core/bitstreams/1891cb2b-f7de-5e37-a40f-66e34728144d/content.

World Institute of Sustainable Energy (2017), "Renewables India 2017: Toward Grid Parity, Status of RE Development in India in 2016–17", World Institute of Sustainable Energy, Pune.

World Trade Organisation (2013), "Aid for Trade at a Glance 2013: Connecting to Value Chains", Geneva.

Yépez, A., A. Levy, A. M. Valencia J. (2016), "The Energy Sector: opportunities and challenges", Energy Division, Inter-American Development Bank, https://publications.iadb.org/en/publications/english/viewer/The-Energy-Sector-Opportunities-and-Challenges.pdf

Yhome, K. (2017), *'Acting East' through India's subregions*. ORF Occasional Paper, No. 123, New Delhi: Observer Research Foundation.

Yhome, K. and T.S. Maini (2017), "Regionalism: SAARC and Beyond". ORF Occasional Paper 135, https://www.orfonline.org/wp-content/uploads/2017/12/ORF_OccasionalPaper_135_Regionalism_Yhome.pdf.

Yue, Chia Siow and Yuan, Lee Tsao (1993), "Subregional Economic Zones: A New Motive Force in Asia-Pacific Development", in C. Fred Bergsten and Marcus Noland, eds., *Pacific Dynamism and the International Economic System*. Washington, D.C.: Institute for International Economics, p. 226.

Zee News (2007), "India ready to accept asymmetrical responsibilities: Pranab", June 3, 2007, http://zeenews.india.com/home/india-ready-to-accept-asymmetrical-responsibilities-pranab_374949.html.

Index